W9-DFR-985

HOW TO FIRE
AN EMPLOYEE

HOW TO
FIRE AN EMPLOYEE

by Daniel T. Kingsley

Facts On File Publications
New York, New York ● Bicester, England

CARNEGIE LIBRARY
LIVINGSTONE COLLEGE
SALISBURY, N. C. 24144

120911

HOW TO FIRE AN EMPLOYEE

Copyright © 1984 by Daniel T. Kingsley

All rights reserved. No part of this book may be reproduced or utilized in any form or by any means, electronic or mechanical, including photocopying, recording or by any information storage and retrieval systems, without permission in writing from the Publisher.

Library of Congress Cataloging in Publication Data
    Main entry under title:

Kingsley, Daniel T.
    How to fire an employee.

    Includes index.
    1. Employees, Dismissal of.
HF5549.5.D55H68   1983   658.3'13   82-25140
ISBN 0-87196-247-0

Printed in the United States of America

10   9   8   7   6   5   4   3   2

Contents

1. Ready on the Firing Line — 1
2. The Psychology of Dismissal — 19
3. Considerations of Seniority — 44
4. Considerations of Performance — 49
5. Considerations of Behavior — 62
6. Alternatives to Dismissal — 72
7. Outplacement Assistance — 90
8. Appealing the Termination — 107
9. Discrimination and the Courts — 119
10. A Guide to Successful Termination — 156

CHAPTER 1

Ready on the Firing Line

DON RILEY SAT at his desk in an unusual state. He was trembling and nauseated. He glanced at the clock on the wall. It was two minutes to four. Already he could hear cars starting up in the parking lot, making their early Friday afternoon getaways for the weekend. He knew he must get on quickly with the distasteful job at hand.

There was no way around it. Randy White, his assistant, was not pulling his own weight in the company anymore. He had simply become a victim of corporate burnout. Riley and White had been working together for over ten years. In fact, White had brought Riley into Atlas Industries when the job of marketing director had suddenly opened up with the retirement of the former chief.

Yet Riley could no longer plead ignorance of White's situation. Department morale was sinking. But the crucial point had to do with corporate profits. Because marketing was off, the department's overhead was heavy. The company president told Riley to reduce the clerical support staff by 15 percent. Moreover, the president cautioned Riley that middle management might need some careful scrutiny and review. In all cases, the targets for the reduction in force and any other personnel alterations were up to Riley.

Although seniority considerations dictated most of the people Riley would terminate from the clerical staff, the management considerations were a bit trickier. Riley finally admitted to himself that Randy White, though Riley's closest friend, had been

1

slacking off noticeably and increasingly over the past year and a half. Despite the fact that White had seniority on Riley, it *had* to be done. To keep his own job, Riley had to fire his best friend! It was the worst dilemma he had ever faced.

Why did he have to be the one to give Randy White the ax? Couldn't, in this one instance, the president intercede? Riley's whole nature rebelled against administering such a coup de grace. He had lain awake for three nights now. There was simply no tomorrow.

There was a great deal of guilt he could not quite account for. *He* had not caused Randy White to burn out—that was White's fault, if indeed it was anyone's fault. There was no logical reason for Riley to feel guilty. Other people were capable of firing subordinates without going through this mea culpa syndrome. Why couldn't he?

Case History Number 1: Randy White

It was now four o'clock. Riley pulled himself together and rang up Randy White. In a moment White was sitting opposite him, leaning back in the chair stifling a Friday-afternoon yawn. Riley was finding it difficult to speak.

"I'm ready to take off for the marina," White said. "I'm surprised you're still hanging around the office, Don."

Riley plunged thankfully through the loophole White had offered him. Anything to avoid facing the problem head on. "How's the boat these days, Randy? I haven't been out with you for years."

"Anytime, pal. Just ask."

"Well . . ." Riley bit his lip. He knew he had to get the conversation headed toward the grim subject. "Sometime soon, Randy. Look." He cleared his throat. "This isn't going to be easy. You know our marketing picture has been getting bleaker by the day."

"So has everybody's," White said.

Riley plowed on doggedly. "The truth of the matter is that

you haven't really been able to perform the way you used to, Randy."

White was very silent, his face suddenly pale. He had apparently sensed what was on Riley's mind.

"I've got to let you go," sighed Riley. "We're going to be losing money this year for the first time since I've been here. Your work simply isn't up to standard. You're through, Randy."

Stunned, White sat looking at his superior. Then his face turned beet red. "I don't believe it, Don! I brought you into this company! I recruited you for the boss. And this is the way you treat me?"

Riley squirmed in his chair. "You've got a wonderful reputation in the field," he said, knowing he was lying a little to ease the blow. "You won't find it hard to get a job."

White sat back and thought. "How much notice do I get?"

"This is it," Riley said.

"Today?"

"You get two weeks' pay. Plus severance."

"How much is that?"

"They've got it all laid out down in finance."

"Can't I use the office for a while? Phone calls? Résumés? Letters?"

Riley hadn't thought about that. He was so relieved to have gotten through the crucial part of the interview that he quickly gave White permission to use the office for as long as he needed in his job-hunting activities.

A moment or two later Riley ushered out the stunned former employee and was ringing up Arthur Mason. As he waited for Mason to come into the office, Riley leaned back in the chair and sighed with relief. He had felt more guilt over Randy White's termination than he should have. The rest of the layoffs would be much easier . . . he thought.

Case History Number 2: Arthur Mason

Next on the list was Arthur Mason. Mason was one of the company's junior executives being groomed for "better things."

However, he was a careless worker and a bully. He had become involved in a number of fights with his co-workers. No one had ever caught him in the act, but the word usually got around afterward.

Although his reports were consistently inaccurate, Mason never made any big errors. Most of his mistakes were caught when his figures were included in other reports. His personality and attitude were his most offensive characteristics.

Riley had been surprised when he looked over the rather skimpy performance sheets he kept on his employees to find that Mason was usually evaluated positively and had never been reprimanded for his negative attitude, his carelessness, or his belligerence. However, Riley knew that the company's performance records were usually whitewashes and did not really say exactly what they should have said.

Even though Riley was upset and annoyed over his interview with Randy White, he felt a slight glow of almost sadistic pleasure when he told Mason that he was through at Atlas.

"You can't fire me!" Mason shot back without even letting Riley finish the little set speech the was making.

"Even if earnings were up 500 percent," Riley snapped, "you'd be on the chopping block." His anger was beginning to churn up. "You've never really put your shoulder to the wheel in this organization. It's time you got out."

"This is the twentieth century, Mr. Riley!" Mason sneered. "Shoulder to the wheel, huh?"

Riley flushed at his own outdated metaphor. "I was mistaken in hiring you in the first place," he said slowly. "And when I found out how mistaken I was, I should have fired you immediately."

"I've heard no complaints!" Mason replied, smiling fatuously.

"Consider yourself lucky, then," snapped Riley. "You can leave with a clean slate."

Now Mason lounged back in the chair as if challenging Riley to remove him from the office. "You're afraid to hear the truth about yourself, aren't you?"

Riley was puzzled. "What's *that* supposed to mean?"

Mason laughed. "Oh, come on, now. That's what's behind this—this charade of a termination—isn't it?"

Then Riley remembered that Mason had indeed caused a flap in the front office some months earlier when he had criticized one of the airplane valves Atlas was turning out for an aviation plant. There was even a write-up in the local newspaper about it. But everything had blown over in a very short time. The president had chastized Riley for not taking direct action in reprimanding Mason, but Riley had managed to shrug off the scolding. He had done nothing about it.

"There's nothing behind this termination except your inability to perform up to standard!" fumed Riley.

Mason was about to respond, but Riley cut him off. He instructed Mason to see the finance department for the details of his severance pay, told him to be out of the office by the end of the day, and dismissed him.

Mason continued to watch Riley carefully. Now he stood up and sauntered to the door, where he turned and smiled back at Riley. "I know a lot about Atlas products," he mused. "Detweiler would like to find out some things. Maybe you'll be sorry you got rid of me when I peddle Atlas's secrets to them."

Riley blew up. "I doubt that your attention span is adequate to give you any real understanding of our secrets, *Arthur*. Maybe if you'd paid a little more attention to your work you *could* tell them something. I wouldn't give you a wooden nickel for any information in that head of yours!"

Turning crimson, Mason stalked through the door, slammed it, and vanished down the corridor.

Case History Number 3: Monica Henry

Monica Henry was a very attractive young woman who had been hired as a secretary in the marketing department about eighteen months earlier. She was the last person hired by Don Riley. Although she had made no trouble during her time of employment, she apparently had some difficulty in writing letters, particularly with her spelling. It took her a long time to look up words in the dictionary. There were grammatical errors in her letters. Riley knew that everyone makes mistakes, but he had heard that she made more mistakes than any of the other secretaries.

The truth of the matter was that Riley was not unaware that the other women in the department were a trifle jealous of Monica Henry. She was younger and prettier than most of them. But when he had decided on the cutbacks in his clerical staff, Riley had checked up on her through other sources. Even the men in the department admitted that she was a bit slow in producing letters and reports for them. And she had no seniority.

Understandably, Riley felt less guilty about firing Monica Henry and the other clerical workers than he did about firing middle-level managers because he could attribute the clerical terminations to a reduction in force. Also, in the specific case of Monica Henry, her youth and her obvious attractiveness would increase her chances of getting a good job somewhere else.

Although he liked Monica Henry, Riley was unacquainted with any of the details of her private life. However, he felt that of all the people in his department, she would be the one to land on her feet with the least effort. All of his other secretaries were older and had seniority over her and actually were more skilled at their jobs than she was.

He approached the termination with a calm that surprised even him. But when he told Monica Henry that she would have to go, her eyes filled with tears, and she began to cry. Riley was stunned. He had never anticipated such a reaction. From Randy White, quite possibly a few four-letter words. But tears! From Monica Henry?

Visibly upset, he fumbled in his pocket for a clean handkerchief, which she took with an apologetic air and wiped her eyes. Watching her, Riley felt like jumping out the window. Nothing was going right today. As he sat there in his misery, she tried to regain control of herself. Riley aged a hundred years watching her.

"I thought I was doing a good job," she said finally, sniffling a bit. She brushed back her long hair and looked at him accusingly. Riley noticed that she had fine dark eyes.

"We've been experiencing declining profits," Riley told her finally. "We're cutting back all along the line. I know you'll do very well somewhere else."

"But I like it here!"

Riley realized he was losing control of the conversation. He tried to think of something reassuring to say, but he had already said all he could.

"Isn't there a place for me in another department?"

Riley smiled. "I've talked to the other department heads," he said tentatively. "But every other job is filled."

Her eyes were watching him steadily. He looked away from her. In fact, he had not discussed her individual situation with anyone else. He had not thought it necessary. Besides, the other departments were cutting back, too.

"I could take a demotion and work on the files," she said.

"It's impossible, Monica!" snapped Riley, realizing she was beating him at his own game and beginning to force him into an untenable position. "You'll simply have to go."

"Today?" Her face stiffened.

"Yes. Report to finance and you'll learn the details of your severance pay and other benefits."

She stood up. He noticed how very attractive she was. But when she looked at him, she was not smiling. In fact, she said nothing at all but turned abruptly and left.

Riley sank back in his chair and smiled thinly. He had a few more to go, but the worst seemed to be over. Every moment of it had been traumatic. Firing people was one of the worst things any manager was required to do. He wished there were some way to do it without the personal pain he had suffered already. He wondered if anyone could ever come up with a foolproof plan to do it without guilt, without recrimination, without emotional stress. He thought not.

He was wrong.

It could be done expertly and efficiently, without occasioning the personal pain—on both sides of the desk—that his handling of the first three situations had caused.

In addition to causing the personal trauma, Don Riley made a number of serious errors in his preparation for and his execution of the three terminations discussed. These mistakes will be identified in later chapters and the correct action indicated.

*   *   *   *

Mark Andrews faced the same unenviable task as Don Riley in his work as an executive at Maddon, Inc.—formerly a small electronic and computer parts company but lately a large manufacturer of personal computers.

After purchasing an ailing computer company and merging with it, Maddon, Inc., had found itself bloated with staff and overhead. An across-the-board reduction in force ensued in the wake of the merger. A number of assembly workers and excess staff in corporate departments were laid off. The entire operation at Maddon was overhauled, and an expanded product line and manufacturing calendar were created.

Despite the streamlining of operations at Maddon, new product orders were far fewer than expected. Moreover, existing quotas for standing orders were late in being met. Productivity estimates showed Maddon production at only 65 percent, and company morale was sagging from the disappointing first quarter profits following the merger.

Concerned, Mark Andrews and his partners, the Maddons, reviewed operations closely. As a result, Andrews found himself in fundamentally the same situation as Don Riley.

Case History Number 4: Jim Young

Andrews knew he had to terminate Jim Young, the head of the manufacturing division of Maddon, Inc. Young had gone to work for Maddon when it was a small and struggling manufacturer of computer parts and electronic items. That was fifteen years ago. A hardworking man, Young was one of the first employees hired by Andrews, who owned the company along with the two Maddon brothers. Young was put in charge of the manufacturing division. At the time, there were fifteen employees under him.

Young thrived on work. He was the perfect supervisor. He knew the small parts manufacturing business, and he was a good person to have around. He could do everything he expected his subordinates to do.

With the boom in the computer industry, Maddon, Inc., began to grow by leaps and bounds. Soon the company was not only manufacturing computer parts but was also developing its own personal computer. Within ten years, Young was in charge of a hundred people rather than just fifteen. Five years later, his division had expanded to two hundred.

Young was made vice-president of the manufacturing division. He was now fifty years old. He had been thirty-five when he joined Maddon. By now he had become quite set in his ways. He liked the camaraderie of the shop; he liked to work on the line with the machine operators. Individually, he was very good with the workers.

As the company grew, the plant did not seem able to keep up with its increasing production quotas. Young supervised a half dozen foremen, one running each section of the greatly expanded division. But he still liked to drop in and work on the line. One foreman complained that Young did not delegate proper authority to any of his foremen. He wanted to do it all himself.

The computer industry continued its meteoric expansion. As company after company jumped in to compete, several were forced out of business. One of these new computer companies, Sylvester Industries, had developed a personal computer that was a marvel, but sudden personal conflicts among top management prompted the firm to reorganize. As a result, profits dropped, and it was put up for sale.

When Maddon, Inc., which formerly supplied parts for Sylvester, purchased the company outright, it was considered industrywide the perfect acquisition. Maddon was in a position of great potential. It could perhaps become one of the big names in the computer industry.

But production had been suffering for some years now. Before the purchase of Sylvester, being a few days or a few weeks behind in production quotas was not a crucial matter. Now it was.

Andrews had studied the situation long and hard. It all came down to Jim Young. Andrews and the Maddons liked Young, always dealt with him personally. The families of the four men were close. But Andrews knew that in spite of the fact that Young had helped build the company, he was now in over his head. He simply was unable to delegate authority to get things moving faster.

It was essentially a situation in which an employee with excellent performance potential had gradually been overtaken by events and by complications totally out of his control. He did not change as circumstances changed around him. He was an anachronism. He had to go.

Early one Tuesday morning, Andrews called Jim Young into the conference room. He had a folder in front of him, which he opened as Young came in and sat down.

Without any preamble, Andrews got to the point. "Jim, I have disturbing news for you. However, once you realize the import of the proposed change, I'm sure you'll understand and make the best of it."

Young was watching his superior carefully. "I know about the problem in my department. I've been trying to work out something. Do you have a solution?"

Andrews shook his head. "It's a whole new ball game, Jim. We've grown too fast. It's not easy to accept that much change all at once. You've been here from the beginning. You built the company with us. But you have to go. The department you head simply isn't keeping up. We've discussed this in the past, yet quota schedules have never been later than they have these past six months."

Young winced. "I'm sorry."

"We want to help you," said Andrews. "In the next room there's a man named Ronald Simpson. He's what is called an outplacer. He'll tell you how to prepare yourself for a job hunt, and he'll help you until you find work."

Young bit his lip. "How long do I have here, Mark? If I could stay a week or two . . ."

"You leave within two hours, Jim," said Andrews. "I'm sorry, but that's the way it is. You'll simply clean out your desk after you've talked with Simpson and go with him."

Young's face was pale, but he seemed determined to make the best of this expected blow. "Right."

Andrews stood up behind the table, extending his hand. "Good-bye, Jim. It's been a real pleasure working with you through all these years. I'm sorry it had to end this way."

They shook hands. Young was noticeably upset.

Andrews picked up the folder, tucked it under his arm, and led Young through the side door of the conference room into the room adjoining. In there Ronald Simpson waited for Young. No one in the office knew who Simpson was or why he was there. That was all part of the outplacement plan.

Andrews introduced Young to Simpson and waited a moment as they sat down at the table between them and started talking.

Then Andrews closed the door to the room and returned to his office. Outplacement was the only answer for the Jim Young problem, he realized. It was a most modern, most clear-cut, most impersonal way to accomplish termination. For those in the high echelons of business—in the $30,000-a-year-and-up category—it was the only way to go.

He had wished Young luck and knew that Young would be getting the best advice available from the outplacer the company had hired to lead him through the next few crucial months.

Case History Number 5: Dick Barton

After Young's termination, a new man was brought in from a large, progressive manufacturing concern. Young's job was phased out and a new one created to make maximum use of the new man's talents at increasing productivity. Within four months, he had accomplished the virtual eradication of the backlog of Maddon's manufacturing quotas. Production was working at such a rate, in fact, that a greater volume of orders could be processed than originally forecast. Yet, while orders for traditional Maddon products continued to come in steadily, the new product lines were moving much slower than anticipated. More orders would have to be generated to keep the manufacturing division in work.

After much consideration, Mark Andrews concluded that the problem with new product orders was more a function of poor promotion than of poor sales effort. Inadequate support was offered from corporate communications to these new products, and Dick Barton, director of corporate communications, was the responsible party.

Dick Barton was in his thirties, a pale, thin, and underdeveloped man but very witty and personable. He had grown up in the slums of a large eastern city and done well as an advertising account executive. He came out to the Midwest to Maddon, Inc., to get away from the urban environment.

Although he was a college dropout, he had become a brilliant writer with good business sense. For a while he worked as assistant director in Maddon, Inc.'s, advertising department and soon was put in charge. His talents were extensive, and his work was appreciated deeply by the Maddon brothers and by Andrews. With the Sylvester merger, the advertising department grew into a larger corporate communications department with Barton as director.

But Barton's psychological and physical profiles were spotty. After he had been at Maddon eighteen months, he suddenly disappeared and did not resurface for ten days. When he did reappear, he looked as if he had been put through some kind of medieval torture. This disappearing act happened again about a year later and then with increasing frequency. Finally, the nurse at Maddon suspected that Barton's problem was linked to drug abuse.

About three months before the Sylvester deal was sealed, Barton was put on a methadone maintenance program for drug withdrawal. At the time, he admitted that he had been on and off drugs for years in the city but had thought he was recovered when he moved to the Midwest. He had been forced to leave college because of his drug problem.

During treatment, Barton produced work of excellent quality, though his behavior remained somewhat unpredictable. He would vanish from the office and wander around for hours before returning. Just before a deadline or major appointment, he sometimes disappeared. He relied on his assistant, Laurie Petersen, a young woman in her twenties, to finish material or meet with press contacts and colleagues.

After three such disappearances, Barton was warned and seemed to straighten out. Then Barton disappeared again on the day before a major computer industry convention. He called in asking his assistant to fill in for him as usual. However, Laurie Petersen had an abscessed tooth that had to be attended to, and she could not possibly direct the Maddon exhibit at the convention.

By then, Andrews had decided that despite Barton's talent, he was too unreliable to get the new product promotions successfully launched. No matter how talented a person might be, if unable to do the assigned job, he or she was useless to the company—and, in fact, could be a detriment to smooth operations.

When called into the conference room by Mark Andrews, Dick Barton sat in the chair, looking shrunken and older than his age. Andrews felt sad about him. He said, "Dick, I'm sorry this hasn't worked out. Your evaluation sheets show that you are a worker with his heart in the right place, but you are simply unable to perform with the consistency that we need at this company. When you disappeared two weeks ago, there was insufficient staff prepared for a major convention. You know this is your responsibility. Along with your reliability, your attendance is also a major problem."

Barton nodded. "You're going to fire me, of course."

"I have to, Dick. You simply can't handle the work. You've forced Laurie Peterson into difficult situations. You've accumulated numerous unauthorized absences. If we always need a backup person to take charge when you're gone, what's the use of having you? Beyond that, we need more—not less—effort from communications to get the new products moving."

"I have this psychological problem." Barton grimaced as he uttered this euphemism for drug addiction.

"We've tried to help you cope with it."

"I thought the government had a disability law. I thought it prevented companies from firing someone with a drug problem."

Andrews smiled. "You'd make a good guardhouse lawyer. The government *does* have a disability law. However, it doesn't cover a person on methadone or on drugs who is constantly vanishing and forcing other workers to do the job for him or her."

Again, Andrews had done his homework. Barton knew his rights, to an extent. Government statutes did indeed protect the "handicapped" or "disabled," but only in certain ways. A drug addict could be considered handicapped by his or her drug "disability." As such the addict could be protected from termination for that reason alone.

However, because of a quirk in the law, a drug addict in a methadone treatment program is considered not yet rehabilitated and therefore not under the protection of the Rehabilitation Act.

In the case of Dick Barton, the principal point was that his behavior was a threat to the morale of those working around him while he was in his present state of withdrawal treatment. That, coupled with the crucial need to boost sales promotion of new products, motivated Andrews to fire him. The legal point was simply a consideration Andrews had been forced to study in implementing his decision to terminate.

Barton seemed to accept what Andrews was saying, and Andrews went on.

"You'll be getting three weeks' severance pay," he said, looking down at a paper in front of him. "You'll also be getting a lump sum of accumulated profit sharing. It's all spelled out in the severance package on this sheet I'll give you later.

"You'll also be getting group health insurance, life insurance, and dental coverage until the end of the month, at which time these will be phased out, and you'll be responsible for paying for them yourself." Andrews glanced up. "Health insurance is expensive, Dick. I do hope you get a job soon.

"There will be other perks as well. For example, for anyone in your kind of job, the company sets aside office space and secretarial help for you during the time you are job hunting. You'll be able to use office space and secretarial aid in preparing your résumés for a period of three weeks, one week for each year of your employment. Is that clear?"

"Yes, sir, and I appreciate it."

"At the end of the three weeks, you'll have to wind up your activities in the office. However, you'll still be able to have telephone messages taken here. They will be relayed to you when you phone in. You'll be able to have messages taken here for another three weeks. In that way you won't have to tell anyone during that period that you're not actively employed."

"That sounds fine," said Barton.

"Laurie Petersen will be taking over your position. During your three weeks, I expect you to be on hand to answer any questions she might have about the job. However, I don't want you to think you have to do any work during that time. Simply be on hand to answer queries if they are asked. It's an imposition, perhaps but since we are allowing you to use the facilities, we feel it is an even quid pro quo."

Barton agreed to the terms.

"You've had the use of the company car for three years whenever you've had to travel to the printers or the engravers. That privilege will continue for your three weeks. If you need to use the car, though, I want you to check first with Laurie Petersen to make sure she doesn't need it for the time you intend to use it. Your gasoline credit card will be yours to use until your three weeks' severance is up, at which time you'll have to turn it in."

Andrews looked over the papers carefully. "You'll be able to use me and anyone else here at Maddon as a reference. You may be sure we won't be unfair to you if any prospective employer calls to ask about your abilities."

Andrews leaned back in the chair. "You'll need to know how we're going to handle the news of your leaving. It's what we call a 'cover story.' "

"I thought you'd just say I was a junkie and couldn't hack it here."

Andrews smiled. "Nobody knows you're on methadone, Dick. That's right, isn't it?"

"I don't think anybody knows."

"Then let's not give them a chance to put you down for drug addiction. We'll say we terminated you for excess absenteeism and unavailability on the job. How do you feel about that? Does it strike you as a feasible cover story?"

Barton nodded. "I can certainly live with that."

"We'll put out a memo to that effect as soon as possible."

Andrews then handed Barton the folder listing his severance pay and benefits and stood up to signal the end of the interview. Barton rose and shook hands. Andrews felt a pang of sorrow as he watched the departing figure of the obviously sick man. He sat at the table a few minutes after Barton had gone, pondering this dismissal. He had been forced to act to forestall the inevitable slump in morale that would eventually have resulted from Dick Barton's repeated and flagrant absences from the job.

Yet he did not like what he had had to do. But then, of course, no one really relished a dismissal. It was the most difficult part of any manager's job to terminate an employee—even someone who deserved it.

Case History Number 6: Mary Healy

A few weeks after the Barton termination, Mark Andrews found himself yet again calling in an employee for termination. This time, though, it was with little sadness. It was a case of the last straw with Mary Healy, who, it seemed, was a sweet talker during an interview and a grave problem in the office.

Mary Healy was late for her appointment with Andrews. He was not surprised. Mary was usually late, or early, or absent altogether from most appointments. A belligerent 28-year-old with the sharpest tongue Andrews had ever encountered, Healy had been a troublemaker from the instant she had been hired at Maddon, Inc.

"Ah, Mary," Andrews said with a smile when she finally came in. "Would you please sit down?"

The woman's green eyes glared at him. "I'd prefer to stand."

"Oh, very well," Andrews said easily. "Mary, it has come to my attention that you have been absent once again for over two weeks."

"Ten days. I was sick," Healy said softly. She eased herself into the chair opposite Andrews.

"Two weeks," Andrews said firmly, glancing at the folder in front of him for confirmation." And evidently you've not seen a doctor—at least, you haven't filed for medical reimbursement."

"I had the flu. I didn't need to see a doctor."

"You seem rather unconcerned, Mary. Two weeks is hardly an insignificant absence."

"So what of it?"

Andrews reviewed a paper in front of him. "Unfortunately, there is no scoring on the evaluation sheet for impudence. Only for attitude, in which I see you have hit a new low with us; personal efficiency, which I see is nonexistent in your case; interpersonal relations, in which I find you 'remarkably lacking in cooperation'; and dependability, one of our first zeros."

Healy sat smugly.

"This still fails to concern you?"

"It's all a lot of trash."

Coolly, Andrews thumbed through the thick folder. "Mary, you've finally exhausted all your known disciplinary resources." He ticked them off on his fingers: "One, reprimand, verbal. Two, counseling. Three, first written reprimand. Four, first appeal. Five, second written reprimand. Six, second appeal. Seven, third written reprimand. Eight, third appeal. Nine, final warning."

He paused, looking up at her.

"You've gone through all the possible steps in our appeal procedure, Mary. You have consistently and blatantly refused to obey the rules here concerning absenteeism. I must therefore tell you that you are being terminated as of today. You have two weeks' severance pay, which you can pick up at finance. You will be off the premises by the end of the day. In addition to your two weeks' severance pay, you will be allowed one week's pay for the year you have worked here." Andrews smiled thinly. "Although, judging from your record here, you haven't really put in much of that year on the job."

Healy laughed. "You can't fire me, Mr. Andrews."

"Sorry to contradict you, Mary. I have just done so."

"I'll file a complaint with the labor counsel."

"You're not a member of the union, Mary. Nor do we have a contract."

"They'll fight my case."

"Even if they would, you have no case." Andrews tapped the folder in front of him. "*I* have the case." He ticked the contents off on his fingers. "One, a copy of the original memorandum of the initial counseling session. Two, copies of all the reprimands. Three, a list of performance shortcomings to be improved—which were not. Four, the specific period of time set in which you were to correct your performance—which you did not. Five, a statement that you had one more chance to bring your performance up to date. Six, a copy of my warning to you. I think that wraps it up, Mary—all dated, signed, and witnessed."

"It's obvious you're firing me with malicious intent." Healy was eyeing him intently. "You don't like me because I refused to go out on a date with you."

"*I* asked you out on a date?"

"Come on, Mark."

"Mr. Andrews," came the equable reply.

"Who's to say you didn't try to date me, Mark? It's your word against mine."

Andrews smiled. "It's all over, Mary. You're through. I am handing you a folder containing the details of your severance package and other pertinent information you may need."

"Do I get a reference, Mr. Andrews?" Healy asked sweetly.

"You can use anyone at the company as a reference," Andrews told her. "Be assured that whoever it is will tell the truth about you."

Healy laughed.

"We'll post you here as having been terminated for excess absenteeism and unsatisfactory performance because of it." Andrews glanced up. "I think that's all. Good-bye, Mary."

Healy stood up suddenly, hands flat on the table, leaning forward. "You haven't heard the last from me, you hear that?"

"I think I have, Mary." He stood up opposite her, his gaze unflinching.

For a moment the two of them stared at each other. Then Healy relaxed and turned toward the door. At the door she took one parting shot:

"Hey, I can get you on 'implied contract.' When I was hired, you promised me I could work here as long as I wanted."

"Only if your performance warranted it," Andrews said softly.

She glared at him a moment, then stomped out.

Andrews sat down again. He had prepared his case against her to the last meticulous detail. He knew he would never hear from her again. He was right.

*   *   *   *

Both Don Riley and Mark Andrews were performing tasks they did not like. The fact that Riley handled his three terminations all wrong and Mark Andrews handled his all correctly does not alter the truth of the matter—the terminator suffers during a termination as much as the terminatee.

The suffering is different, but it is psychologically as intensive and as painful to both parties to the termination drama— the protagonist and the antagonist.

In order to determine the best possible psychological approach to a termination, especially from the standpoint of the terminator, it is necessary to analyze not only the emotional reactions of the person to be fired but also those of the person doing the firing. In addition, the emotional reactions of the people in the company itself will have to be studied and assessed.

Once an understanding of these difficult emotional traumas is reached, it will finally become evident that there is a way to terminate with a minimum of pain, remorse, and guilt.

CHAPTER 2

The Psychology of Dismissal

TERMINATION is essentially a kind of psychological disaster area no matter whom it touches in business. No matter how many times a terminator terminates, the pain lingers on. No matter how many times a terminatee is terminated, the agony of the scene remains fixed in the memory. No matter how many times terminations occur in departments and offices, the trauma affects other employees indirectly involved in the drama of dismissal.

A Three-Level Disaster Area

On all three levels—that of the terminator, the terminatee, and the co-workers—there can be psychological damage if a termination is not carried out effectively and gracefully. In the case of one that is not, such injurious and lingering aftereffects as those discussed below may be expected.

The Terminator (Don Riley)

"I had been brooding for months over how to get rid of Randy White. Corporate burnout? That was the euphemism I used.

Randy had brought me into the company, I'll grant him that. I was his boss, and he began *using* me as an umbrella for protection from above. He got to be the laziest goof-off in the shop. I tried to warn him, but he was either too thick to understand or thought I was kidding. Yet firing him was a real trauma. My God—fire my best friend?

"Almost instantly, I felt a deep resentment surface. I was head of the department, sure, but why couldn't personnel handle the responsibility of selecting those to go? What right did management have to lay the burden of termination on me? It was a nasty trick. One that annoyed me.

"By the time I got back to my office, I had sunk into a kind of cataleptic trance. I saw only my own shortcomings. If I could have warned Randy about the situation, maybe . . . If I had been any good, perhaps I could have prevented his dismissal. How the hell could he survive once he was let go? I knew his wife so well; I knew the kids. What would they think of it—of *me?*

"I started to panic. I *couldn't* fire Randy White! I had to cover up some way. Fire somebody else, move Randy into that vacant job, hire someone for my assistant. I remember getting up from the desk and peering out the window with my hands clasped behind my back, like an actor in a scene from one of those doomsday dramas when there's a big crisis in the making—the crash of 1929, Pearl Harbor, Watergate.

"Then I realized immediately that none of this was my fault *or* Randy's. Why not put the blame where it belonged? Right on management's head! If the company had any smarts, it would have been able to ride out this recession. It's the little guys— like us—who always have to pick up the pieces when the bridge falls down. Resentment, anger, downright hatred, surfaced in me, and I realized it was all directed at the corporate monster whose shadow seemed to hover over me.

"But that was a momentary feeling. I knew it was usually easiest to blame the colossus—in other words, to vary the metaphor, to bite the hand that feeds you. It was too simple an answer to a complex problem. It wasn't the company that was at fault. How could an impersonal corporate entity cause such emotional trauma in me?

"No. I had already zeroed in on the real culprit. It was Randy White—not the president, not national economy, not the company. *Randy* was the person I most resented. If he had kept up with the job requirements—if he had worked hard, if he had done what he should have done within his job parameters—there wouldn't have been any need to fire him! He was the bad guy. He was the one giving me all the trouble.

"And that was the gamut of emotions I ran through before I buckled down to face the coming ordeal. I loved the guy—but I hated him. My best friend—the man I had to fire. Just what do you say to your best friend when you're about to administer the coup de grace?"

The Terminatee (Randy White)

"I was out in the parking lot sitting in my car before it really hit me. I wasn't watching some kind of Broadway play—I was living the damned thing! Don Riley had really, truly, 100 percent fired me! But I hadn't yet absorbed the idea—the total concept—until I was out of the office and trying to figure our what had happened. It was the kind of shock you get when you hear a good friend or close relative has died. Or when you hear that you've got only a week to live!

"But what made me *livid* was the fact that Don Riley was the one who told me to get out! Don Riley, the guy I brought into the company because I felt sorry for him. It wasn't *all* his fault, of course. It was also the president's. I had never thought much of him. A third-rater. They were all third-rate; the company, for God's sake, was third-rate. And yet *I* was the one going. I was so mad . . .

"Then I realized that quite possibly Don Riley had mistaken the president's intentions. It wasn't *me* he wanted to fire. It was Gus Lingus or someone else. Hell, that was the problem. Somebody got their signals crossed. I felt a surge of self-righteousness. At the same moment I felt the urge to be bighearted about the mistake when it was finally explained to me. Yeah. I'd be big about it.

"I drove home in that state of euphoria, but by the time I got in the front door I knew that there was no mistake. I knew there had been complaints about my work. I remembered the president's warning to me. Feeling lousy, I went out in the backyard and sank down into a lawn chair. Eve was playing bridge next door. I felt hung over without even having had a drink. Life was all over. I could never move again.

"By the time Eve had started dinner, I was in a real fighting mood once again. I told her what had happened. She was shocked—didn't believe it at first. I told her grimly that it was true, all right, that my good friend Riley the Knife had sunk the blade in and that it was all over. Eve tried to calm me down with a drink or two, and for a time it worked. I more or less went into a kind of hibernation.

"But on Saturday morning I was bouncing back. I telephoned the president and told him off in no uncertain terms. He didn't say much. I found myself yelling at him and calling him a lot of four-letter words, and that made me madder than ever. I hung up on him and began calling my friends in the company, telling them what a raw deal they gave me. Then I got in touch with other friends in other companies and told them what a lousy place I had once worked for. Oh, it was quite a day!"

The Co-worker (Gus Lingus)

"Betty Jane came back from the ladies' room in a state of real excitement. She told me that Randy White had been fired and that Monica Henry had been sacked, too.

"I worked directly with Randy White—under him, really—and I knew that things weren't going all that well in the marketing department. I was paralyzed with sudden terror. What if I was next? I stared at the papers in front of me and tried to *think*. Had I been called in to see Don Riley? Had Betty Jane failed to inform me that I was next on the carpet?

"I couldn't concentrate on my work, only on the upheaval. Rather than sit in my office, I left for the day. On Saturday Randy called me early in the morning. He was so high I thought he was drunk. He wasn't. He was simply letting off steam about the company. When he hung up I slumped on the couch with relief. It wasn't me, after all. He was the one to go. I sauntered in to talk to Edna, and she was stunned when I suddenly took her to bed and made love to her.

"I began to sympathize with Randy White. He was in his forties. He'd have a hell of a time landing a big job somewhere else. It was the kind of thing no one wanted to see happen. But actually Randy had been getting away with murder at Atlas. In fact, I had been forced to mend a lot of his fences for him. He had no cause to feel too put upon. In any other company, he'd probably have been let go a lot sooner.

"By the time Monday rolled around, I had become fairly philosophical about Randy's dismissal. My only concern was about the quality of his replacement. After all, I had to work with the newcomer. Would some hotshot come in, take a look around, and roll all the rest of us out one by one to bring in a fresh stable?

"Those of us who were left in the department began huddling together by the water cooler. By about eleven o'clock the consensus was that Randy White had been asking for it for a long time and that things would improve once his replacement was hired and in position. There was a sense of self-righteousness in the air (I'm not very proud of that), and it seemed that the termination of Randy White would not cause the entire company to sink out of sight but rather would polish up its image and prospects somewhat.

"I was sitting alone at a table in the company cafeteria that noon when Randy White sauntered in and sat directly across from me. He began muttering about his 'best friend,' Don Iscariot Riley, and how surprised he was at his betrayal. I tried to sympathize but found myself looking over my shoulder to see who was watching me. Would I be tainted by my contact with this loser? Randy spent the entire meal grousing about the raw deal he had got, talking about other prospects he already had, and suggesting I get myself another job at some company that had a little compassion, respect, and decency in its personnel practices.

"Was he ever bitter! Atlas had always prided itself on its good image in the industry. I wondered what they were thinking upstairs that day."

*   *   *   *

Feelings of bitterness toward a former employer—much akin to the feelings Randy White had after his inept termination by Don Riley—permeate the ranks of the terminated today and should be anticipated and considered by the terminator. Though the brunt of the psychological distress is always borne by the terminatee, the terminator is affected as well by the implications of having terminated an employee, and the termination has a ripple effect that can often touch the terminatee's former co-workers.

The Traumata of Termination

The intelligent employer now approaches the problem of discharge with a great deal more attention to its psychological impact than in the past. There is good reason for this increase in interest. Given management's current emphasis on considering the employee a "human resource," the loss of a worker is indeed a human resource tragedy for any company.

The psychological damage involved in any termination is threefold:

- There is the damage to the individual being terminated.
- There is the trauma to the psyche of the employer who must perform the surgery.
- There are psychological ramifications that affect the morale of the entire company involved.

Psychological Damage to the Terminatee

Studies by psychologists and labor-management specialists have shown that the level of emotional stress resulting from termination can be equated with the stress level resulting from an individual's being told that he or she is dying of an incurable disease.

Both behavior patterns resemble one another to an astonishing degree:

- First there is the shock of revelation.
- Once that shock is absorbed, anger follows.
- Usually, after the anger passes, the individual becomes obsessed by a conviction that there has been an egregious error, that termination is only a clerical mistake.
- When it is finally ascertained that there is no mistake and

that he or she is indeed out of work, a period of ennui ensues.

- After this interim, there is always a very real danger of an identity collapse, an ego disintegration, or a death struggle with the self.
- Once this roller coaster swing in moods is over, a long period of distress attacks the psyche, plunging the individual into despair.
- Eventually there comes a semblance of resurrection and a restoration of self-confidence.

This last period sometimes entails weeks and months of anguish, while the individual struggles with the harsh realities of the situation until he or she can come to grips with it. Then the "patient" begins to rebuild the ego from its shattered remains. This could be termed the "Humpty Dumpty" phase—putting it all back together again—and ends with the reestablishment of self-esteem and confidence. Once these stumbling blocks are passed, the individual is in a position to channel all personal and professional energies into a constructive effort to return to normal, or as close to normal as is possible under the circumstances.

All these phases, with the exception of the last two, have already been discussed by Randy White in his remarks earlier in this chapter. In the end, he did indeed regain his self-confidence and eventually got another job.

Psychological Damage to the Terminator

The terminator's situation is almost as perilous as the terminatee's, though the behavior pattern is different. The stress usually involves the preliminary steps in preparing for an employee's dismissal. While the employee's stress is usually of an externalized nature—expressed through anger and a desire to strike back—the stress on the employer is usually of an internalized or self-consuming nature.

"The manager finds it distasteful because he's a little superstitious," says one consultant in management placement. "He figures what he does to one of his people today will happen to him later on."

An executive interviewed about termination sums it up: "That's the hardest part, having to tell people you know and respect that 'We don't need you anymore.' You know they need that job, just like I need my job."

Another top executive who had to preside over a large across-the-board termination involving over eight hundred workers and a payroll slash of thirty million dollars recalls that the layoff period was "the most difficult and most emotionally charged situation I've ever been involved in."

The usual chain of emotional mood swings goes something like this:

- First there is the feeling of self-pity when the terminator keeps wondering why he or she has been called on to perform this odious chore.
- Once that feeling has worn off, the terminator usually experiences an inflowing of guilt: guilt that the employee has not been trained into a better worker; guilt that the company's need to cut back reflects negatively on its management.
- When that emotion subsides, the terminator begins to feel compassion for the employee—wondering how the terminated individual will meet the bills, what his or her spouse will think, how he or she will survive.
- Another emotion follows—the desire to do anything possible to retain the employee. This is, in a sense, a cop-out phase; it usually dies down after a time.
- At this point, the terminator's psyche begins to fight back. The first spurt of anger is directed at management, at the terminator's superiors. It is their fault, of course. A sense of *blame* enters the psychological picture.
- When it becomes obvious that no blame can be attached to management for cutting back, the terminator sometimes shifts the blame onto the employee to be fired. The terminator's compassion and anger are in total conflict and eventually neutralize each other.
- At this point the terminator begins to prepare himself or herself for the coming ordeal.
- By the time the termination, or "exit," interview is conducted, the terminator should be in complete control of himself or herself emotionally.

Nevertheless, there is still a great deal of psychological trauma involved from the point of view of the terminator.

In the statement by Don Riley at the beginning of the chapter recalling the events leading up to the termination of Randy White, many of these points were touched upon. Unfortunately for the termination, Riley made a number of mistakes in the execution of the exit interview—mistakes that came back to haunt him and that we'll discuss further on.

Psychological Damage to the Co-Workers

Morale is the most fragile of all the emotional bonds that unite individuals in a common interest. Emotions generally are individualistic; the emotion of morale is collective in nature. Collective emotion is as important in the business area as it is in the social area. It is the morale of a business association that can be damaged or affected by individual or mass terminations.

The manner in which a particular termination is communicated to the numerous individuals who make up the working group determines the positive or negative effect on their morale. If a termination is considered by other employees to be just, the act may help morale. However, if the termination is considered unjust, it may shatter the morale of all the workers in the organization.

There is a general chain of emotional responses that involve each of the third parties to any termination. The responses usually follow in a specific order:

- First there is shock and excitement over the news of the termination.
- Almost immediately there are two more emotional reactions:
  1. Relief that the termination doesn't affect the individual.
  2. Sudden fear that the individual might be next on the list of terminations.
  One of these emotions is a positive flow of feeling (that it's the other person), and the other emotion is a negative flow of feeling (that what happened to the other person might happen to him or her).
- Shortly after the relief/fear roller coaster effect, the third party begins to feel compassion for the terminatee, whether liked or not. Sometimes compassion may be balanced by self-

righteousness: the ousted employee got just what was coming to him or her!
- Soon after this emotion has been revealed and mastered, a new emotional response creeps in. Depending on whether the third party likes or dislikes the person terminated, the emotional response becomes one of anger at the company for firing a "good person" or anger at the "bad person" for making everyone else look bad, too.

Gus Lingus reacted in quite a typical fashion after Don Riley terminated Randy White. He even responded with the fear of being tainted by White's presence when the terminated employee sat down to eat lunch with him in the company cafeteria.

Usually at this point, the shifting emotional scenario begins to resolve itself into a conclusion about the firing itself. The co-worker feels that it is "right" and in the company's best interest (also in his or her own interest, of course) or that it is "wrong" and not in the company's best interest (nor in his or her own interest).

Because esprit de corps is an interacting emotional experience, a feeling about whether the firing was justified or unjustified begins to grow of its own accord and spread from one individual to another. Emotions being evanescent and ephemeral, a dominant collective emotional reaction can overwhelm an individual reaction. Soon the entire group of co-workers shares a common response: morale remains high, or morale plummets.

The direction in which company morale moves is directly linked to the manner in which the employer brings about a termination.

Dos and Don'ts in Dismissal

Because of the enormous importance attached to worker reaction to a termination, the terminator involved in such an action must be able to deal with his or her own personal feelings about the termination. The terminator must be able to accomplish what is required—namely, to terminate objectively and cleanly—without permitting his or her own emotional shadings to cause blurred judgment and clouded motives.

Every termination is an individual case. A gamut of emotional reactions and intensities of emotion is possible. None of these must ever be allowed to interfere with the objective sought.

Three Common Attitudinal Errors

Emotional reactions in the terminator may range from intense anger through great sadness, to almost complete indifference, with nuances of emotions in between.

Anger. A feeling of extreme anger toward the terminatee may overwhelm the terminator when he or she is ordered to dismiss a particular individual. The emotion might well be described like this: "You made me do this by being inefficient. I'm angry with you for putting me in this unpleasant, distasteful position." In truth, the terminator has put himself or herself in the position, not the other way around. The *employee* wants to remain in the job as is.

Note: No terminator has the right to be angry at a terminatee for being what he or she is. The problem leading to termination exists in the employee's failings or in the company's failings and has no place in the mind of the terminator. The terminator must deal with the problem at its source and not allow emotional hang-ups to shade his or her own perceptions and efforts to work it out. Anger has no place in a termination.

Sorrow. A feeling of brooding sorrow may overwhelm the terminator when he or she is obliged to dismiss an individual. Of course, a certain degree of compassion is necessary to assure humane treatment. However, indulgence in compassion and sorrow can be overdone. A feeling of pity and understanding may intensify into a sad and guilt-ridden state of mind that can send erroneous vibrations from terminator to terminatee. If, for example, the sadness becomes too poignant, the terminatee may well get the idea that the terminator is experiencing a sense of guilt; if the appearance of guilt is there, the terminatee may begin to wonder whether there is *reason* for guilt. The next step is for the terminatee to feel that he or she has been put upon, wronged—that the termination is unfair, unjust, and in flagrant violation of objectivity.

Note: A certain tendency toward guilt may be a natural part of the terminator's general psychological makeup. However, *too much* guilt becomes self-defeating by projecting itself upon the terminatee. The terminatee's normal reaction to observation of excessive guilt is to assume that where there's smoke, there's fire—that is, where there's guilt, there's *error*. This is absolutely *not* what the terminator wants to communicate to the terminatee.

Indifference. An attempt to deal with an interview in an objective way sometimes develops into a contest of conflicting desires within the terminator: a desire to be tough and unbending and a desire to be sympathetic and compassionate. The ideal terminator has a well-rounded emotional profile; he or she can be firm while still being sympathetic and compassionate. However, many a terminator fears that his or her own compassion can be taken advantage of by a clever terminatee. Those who are unsure of themselves may put on the stiff-upper-lip facade, the "biting-the-bullet" front, to feign indifference. Unfortunately, indifference is the wrong approach in a situation where rage and tears may result from such a stone-faced attitude.

Note: Some observers call this the "hardness syndrome" in our society—"a pressure that dictates that a manager be tough and fearless, that he or she accept no nonsense." It is, unfortunately, too prevalent in the disciplinary area of business and has become a negative stereotype. Stony indifference is not to be condoned in the termination interview; the usual result is alienation and personal rage at the company. In turn, this is bad for morale and bad for the public image of the organization.

Four Attitudinal Musts

Any termination promises to be a dialogue fraught with emotion and outbursts of feeling. The terminator involved in the dialogue must anticipate shock, anger, and perhaps even tears as the interview progresses. It is most important for the terminator to understand and control his or her own emotions when handling the interview. If the terminator does not, he or she is quite apt to lose control of the dialogue itself.

The terminator must watch out for his or her own emotional excesses, keep anger under control—if any is felt—and never allow compassion to degenerate into a guilt-ridden demeanor that might give the terminatee the impression that the firing is unjust. The terminator must also avoid being cold and aloof to an extent that arouses rage.

His or her own demeanor should indicate to the terminatee that:

- The terminator is sorry about having to terminate the employee, but it must be done.
- He or she has compassion and empathy for the employee but does not intend to play the bleeding heart nor imply that there is something wrong with the termination.
- He or she does not consider the employee a criminal and will help in any reasonable way.
- He or she does not place blame for the termination on anyone—neither the employee nor the company's higher-ups.

Analysis of Right and Wrong Attitudes

In case history number 2 in our opening chapter, we noted that Don Riley fell into one of the most dangerous of all traps when he was terminating Arthur Mason. Because he did not actually like Mason personally, Riley allowed himself to lose his temper. Compare Riley's performance with the performance of Mark Andrews during his interview with Mary Healy in case history number 6. She was deliberately trying to goad him into losing his temper, but he remained calm.

If Andrews felt anger—and he most likely did—he never let it show. If he had, he would have lost control to Mary Healy and her defiant and challenging attitude. In fact, it was Riley's inability to hold Mason in line that goaded Mason into an action that resulted in a later lawsuit against Atlas Industries. We'll discuss that later.

Again, Riley's emotional response to Monica Henry's sudden outburst of crying in case history number 3 was ragged and unprofessional. For some reason, Riley had never anticipated that she might start crying. He should at least have contemplated such a reaction. In addition, he should have anticipated that Mason would try to goad him. He was totally unprepared for responses of any kind, even though he had brooded over the interviews for days.

Contrast Riley's performance with that of Mark Andrews. Andrews had anticipated trouble from everyone. However, the trouble from Jim Young was bound to be minor, because any reaction would be the responsibility of the outplacer in charge. With Mary Healy, Andrews anticipated in detail her denials and her charges; he anticipated them so clearly that he had all the facts in front of him, *on paper*, to refute them. And with Dick Barton, case history number 5, he even had the details of the disability statutes in mind clearly enough to explain them.

Note that Andrews closely followed the four positive precepts just described: he did his duty as he had to; he had compassion and empathy for the three employees, but he did not knuckle under to them; he was willing to help in any reasonable way; he accepted the blame for the decision to terminate and admitted it to himself.

As for Riley: because he was ill-prepared, he tried to dodge the terminations from the first; he was angry at Mason and equally angry with Randy White; he did not try to help any of the employees through their traumas; he placed the blame for the termination on the employees themselves—even, to a degree, on his old friend White.

The question obviously arises: Is there any way the average terminator can make the termination process any less painful?

The answer, of course, is yes.

Easing the Pain of Separation

Efforts to minimize the personal and professional trauma suffered by the terminated employee fall into two general categories:

- Cash compensation
- Noncash compensation

Although both types of compensation are geared to benefit the terminatee, cash compensation in the form of severance pay is of crucial importance to the newly jobless worker.

Companies handle settlement arrangements in many different ways. Some have prepared policies based on specific benefits; others make separate deals with each person terminated. In all cases, management should provide a written document for the terminatee so he or she will be assured of getting everything due.

Money has become an increasingly important consideration in the trauma of termination because of the increase in the duration of unemployment between jobs. The average unemployment period rose nearly 500 percent during the first five years of the 1970s. Financial support naturally grows in importance the longer the period of unemployment lasts.

Older workers find it more difficult than younger ones to land a new position after termination. Statistics show that in the 1970s the employee aged fifty-five to sixty-four was out of work for an average of twenty weeks, compared to fifteen weeks for the employee aged twenty to twenty-four. The difficulty usually results from a more limited mobility, an obsolescence of skills, and management's subtle age discrimination.

These factors must be considered by the employer in designing a severance package that will suit each employee and will reflect well on the company. Other employees will be looking hard at the treatment accorded a fellow worker at termination. Sinking morale can be one negative result of a badly planned package.

The main objective of a severance package is to provide a financial bridge to the employee's next job. The problems of a forty-year-old employee with twenty years' service with the company are quite different from those of a sixty-year-old employee with twenty years' service with the company. While service is an important factor, age should be considered as well.

There are five main points in constructing a successful severance package:

- Length of service
- Age
- Unemployment benefits
- Health and life insurance
- Prevailing severance standards

How Length of Service Is Considered

Seniority figures importantly in all union contracts and in most nonunion severance situations with regard to a person's position in a company. The individual who has been working for the longer period of time is, supposedly, more invulnerable to firing. And theoretically, the veteran should reap more benefits if he or she must be terminated.

Severance pay should be related to an employee's length of service as an expression of employer appreciation for loyalty and for past contributions to the firm's success. A study recently made by the Bureau of National Affairs showed that a common formula in large companies is to allot at severance one week's pay for each year's service.

Although this formula is by no means universally adhered to—some employers allot two weeks' pay for every year of service, and others allot less than one—it is a good base figure for a severance pay program.

How Age Should Be Considered

There are many different ways to calculate the importance of the age factor in setting up a severance package. One point to note is the government's decision to use the age of forty as a factor in employment and termination. Statutes written to protect an individual from discrimination by age consider the age of forty the benchmark at which an employee begins to be considered "older."

In recent years age sixty-five has come to be considered as the year retirement starts. At one time mandatory retirement was set at sixty-five. Such is not now the case, with mandatory retirement unacceptable in some instances. However, sixty-five is usually considered in government circles as the end of the line for the work period. Sixty-two is regarded as "early retirement." Social Security figures are based on sixty-five as the age at which benefits begin; sixty-two is the age at which early Social Security benefits start at reduced rates.

One solution to help the out-of-work older person is to give the worker between the ages of forty and sixty-five an extra "allowance" for age at termination—a percentage of payment that can be added to the original base amount of one week's pay for every year's service.

The "allowance" need not be used unless the original base amount, covering the number of years of service, becomes exhausted before the worker gets another job. That is, if the worker has ten years' service, he or she receives the base pay for ten weeks while job hunting; if at the end of that time he or she is still unemployed, the "allowance" factor goes into force.

By assuming that the worker in the top age bracket has twice the trouble locating a new job as the person under age forty, he or she is allocated an allowance of 100 percent of base pay for a specified period in addition to the base severance pay.

By breaking down employee age into five groupings and allotting different percentages of allowance for each, a schedule for the age factor in severance pay might go as follows:

Under 40	0 percent
40–44	25 percent
45–49	50 percent
50–54	75 percent
55–64	100 percent

Thus, if a thirty-five-year-old with ten years' service spent ten weeks looking for work without obtaining it, he or she would receive full pay for ten weeks. Once the ten weeks passed, the former employee would receive no more severance pay.

If a forty-five-year-old with ten years' service were terminated and spent fifteen weeks looking for work before getting it, he or she would receive full pay for ten weeks and would then get an additional 50 percent of the base pay for the five weeks remaining.

A sixty-year-old with ten years' service would receive full pay for ten weeks after termination and would then be paid the same amount for the following ten weeks, providing he or she was still unable to get a job.

Consideration of Unemployment Compensation

A severance package should be set up in such a fashion that an employee need not apply for unemployment compensation immediately upon termination. A person with fifteen years' service would be receiving compensation from the company for a full fifteen weeks; during that time he or she might land another job. If not, the terminated individual would *then* apply for unemployment. In this way, double-dipping—in the employer's pool and in the government's pool—can be avoided.

In turn, this approach protects the employee from the embarrassment of applying for unemployment benefits until his or her company benefits expire.

Consideration of Health and Life Insurance Benefits

Although an employee usually knows the exact amount of cash received for each pay period, he or she does not always realize that there are other, noncash compensations that sometimes amount to over 35 percent of the total cash amount of salary.

This sum may include health and life insurance coverage. Some companies continue to pay health and life insurance benefits during a terminated employee's period of severance. Others do not.

For the person seeking another job, health insurance is extremely expensive in view of the individual's precarious situation, unusual expenses, and worries about the future. The extension of group benefits can help to reduce potentially heavy insurance charges assessed when a departing employee converts to an individual policy.

Health and life insurance benefits have become an important part of any company's benefit package. It is only fair for management to continue paying these costs during the severance period.

In Mark Andrews's exit interview with Dick Barton in case history number 5, he mentioned that health, dental, and life insurance benefits would continue until the end of the month.

Consideration of Prevailing Severance Standards

The arrangements made in the severance package should meet minimum standards prevailing in the community and the industry. The going rate for a comparable severance package in a competing company could be used as a standard for comparison. By adhering to a standard that is known, the employer can be protected from charges of inadequacy by individual non-union employees and from charges by community leaders who might have an ax to grind in portraying the company as anti-worker.

The generosity of a company toward its employees may change from year to year and from economic situation to economic situation. Inflation can cause settlements to escalate over the years; curbing of inflation can cause settlements to become more amenable to management. However, the problem of inflation coupled with economic hardship may actually call for more generous settlements.

The ideal pay package is a difficult one to establish, even with diligent investigation, study, and thought. By following the guidelines suggested here, a reasonable effort can be made toward providing a package that is neither too generous nor too stingy.

One of the main objectives in any severance package is to motivate the terminated employee to locate a new job and settle in quickly. As an incentive for rapid relocation, some companies agree to pay a lump sum if the employee finds a position before the severance package has been completely exhausted.

This lump sum might equal the total amount of the cash compensation that would have been paid to the separated employee during the severance period, minus any cash that has already been paid.

Some Special Termination Perks

Although employees working on a very high level of management usually can arrange for their own job search or, if not, they may be handed over to an outplacer for assistance (as Jim Young was in case history number 4), employees on a lower level will usually go right out and try to get a new job without any help from the company. There is, however, one area of white-collar employment where terminated employees do need all the help they can get. That is the area of middle management.

For the middle manager, there are a number of nonfinancial perks that an employer can provide, including:

- Time
- Office space
- References

The Importance of Time

One of the most essential compensations a terminator can give a terminatee is time. During the severance discussion, the terminator must impress on the terminatee that his or her main purpose is to secure a new job. The terminator should then permit the terminatee to have that time free in order to look around and get résumés printed and distributed.

One temptation for the terminator is to utilize the terminatee around the shop to handle odd jobs that pop up. It is also a temptation to let the terminatee finish up whatever job was being handled at the time of termination. Such a job should be either canceled, postponed, or assigned to someone else.

It is a psychological fact that a terminated employee can find solace in continuing to do the job already being done and pretend that it will last forever. Many people have this blind spot, which enables them to rationalize that such busywork is an adequate substitute for a true job hunt. The terminator should never allow an employee who has been terminated to waste time doing work for the company when he or she should be out looking for another position.

Warning: The terminator must watch out for the terminatee who refuses to go out and look for work. Such an employee may deliberately manufacture new jobs around the office in order to look busy. This is an avoidance of reality.

The Importance of Office Space

As has been said, a middle manager should have an opportunity to use office space and secretarial assistance for conducting a job campaign. However, many small companies do not have the space to provide such help. Secretarial assistance is sometimes strained and inadequate.

One solution to this problem is for the former employer to let the terminatee use the premises only as a telephone number and mail drop, as if he or she were still employed.

Everyone knows that it is easier to get another job if currently employed. The phantom secretary and phantom telephone number are a good solution for a small company that cannot really lend the office space to a terminated employee but wants to help out as much as possible in the separated individual's relocation efforts.

How Long Should Assistance Last?

If the economy is in a normal state, unlike the longer periods of unemployment experienced in the 1970s, the terminated middle manager will get himself or herself rehired within a few weeks or—at most—a month. However, if the economy at large or in a specific field is weak, job hunting may be a drawn-out affair.

The question arises: How long should the company allow the terminated employee to use the premises and/or the office facilities?

Although there is no real rule of thumb for such a limitation, the terminator would not be out of line if he or she allowed the former employee to remain and/or utilize the office facilities about one week for every year of employment—a figure roughly corresponding to the number of weeks' pay allowed in the severance package.

Note: Such a perk is not mandatory. Even for middle managers, many corporations demand immediate exit. There is no set rule, nor does the employee who has been terminated have any legal "right" to remain. This is a perk granted strictly through the generosity and compassion of the company and should be represented as such to the terminatee.

For example, in case history number 5, Mark Andrews told Dick Barton he could have the use of the office facilities for three weeks, one for each of three years of service. Also, if he needed it, he could have the benefit of telephone help for an additional three weeks.

The Importance of References

It is not necessary for a formal severance package to include written references. The old-fashioned type of written accolade of a former employee that was popular at the turn of the century is pretty much a thing of the past. With the telephone in easy reach, a prospective employer can always dial the potential employee's former boss to ask a few pertinent questions about him or her.

However, the terminator should always be fair with the terminatee during the exit interview, especially in explaining why he or she was fired—that is, in naming several shortcomings or areas in which the employee could improve.

This allows the terminatee to prepare his or her own campaign for employment, using the positive factors and minimizing the negative factors.

For example, if the terminatee is aware of being faulted as an ineffective delegator of authority by the terminator, the best course to follow is to tell the prospective employer:

"When you call my former employer, he'll tell you I'm not good at delegating authority. There were certain situations at the company at the time that resulted in a lack of qualified subordinates for certain rather touchy jobs. I simply had to do them myself."

Failure to cope with this issue can result in a traumatic situation for the job hunter. In the words of one former employer:

> When I terminated Roy Henderson, it was a result of his inability to control his underlings. Some people simply aren't tough enough. But Henderson was a sensitive person, and I knew he would have been deeply hurt to learn he was unable to handle people; he thought he was an excellent supervisory type. So I told him that he was being dismissed because of conflicts between him and several members of the board. He didn't get along well with them, either.
>
> When I was called for reference, I had to tell potential employers that Henderson really didn't have the ability to handle people. It took him a long time to get another job. I didn't know that he was basing his whole job campaign on his ability to supervise and on his rapport with people. When I was called for a candid appraisal of him, I always told the truth.
>
> I made a bad mistake. I should have leveled with him. At least he could have prepared his job campaign a little differently. You can do stupid things when you try to cover up your real reasons for terminating people.

It will be recalled that: Mark Andrews did not promise to give Mary Healy any complimentary references when he terminated her in case history number 6. She did not really expect any. But Andrews did promise to give Dick Barton a good reference in his termination interview. A list of company names for references given to Jim Young in case history number 4 was handled by the outplacement assistance agent; Mark Andrews and the outplacer had worked it out ahead of time.

Today a "reference" is usually a person on a higher level than the worker who can give a candid opinion of the worker's performance and comportment if the potential employer wants to seek it out. One reason a written reference is outmoded is the fact that it is usually fabricated by the worker and signed by an indulgent terminator.

Termination without Guilt

It is extremely important for the terminator to be able to communicate to the terminatee during the exit interview the exact amount of severance pay and other benefits due. In the case histories in the first chapter, Don Riley had not done his homework properly and had no idea how much money would be going to Randy White, his longtime assistant, nor to Monica Henry, nor to Arthur Mason. Although not one of them said anything about it, this lack of preparation was offputting to the three terminated employees.

On the other hand, Mark Andrews knew exactly what kind of compensation would be given to Jim Young, to Mary Healy, and to Dick Barton. In fact, he had the details there with him in the folders he later handed to his three former employees.

Don Riley was wrong in allowing Randy White to use the office space "for as long as he needed." Such generosity might seem the compassionate thing to do, given the circumstances, but actually it is never wise to allow such perks to be used on an open-ended basis.

Mark Andrews instructed two of his terminated employees to vacate the premises on the day of termination. The case of Dick Barton, a white-collar worker in middle management, was an exception. But his instructions to Barton were clear, carefully delineated, and fair under the circumstances. His procedure was wiser and less open to abuse than that of Riley.

When Riley allowed Randy White carte blanche to use the office, he was letting his judgment be clouded by his enormous feeling of guilt. It was a mistake he lived to regret, as we shall see.

Anxiety and Self-Hatred

Psychologically, Riley's actions from the beginning were burdened with anxiety and self-recrimination. He allowed himself to prolong the interview needlessly by diving through a loophole presented by the man he was going to terminate. By talking about Randy White's boat, Riley copped out on his own duty to get on with the bad news.

In addition, he allowed the conversation to drag on and on after it could have been wrapped up. He was, in effect, subconsciously trying to forestall the final dropping of the ax on White's neck by keeping him talking. If he had sent White out into the street immediately, Riley would have made the cut cleaner and less painful.

When Riley terminated Monica Henry, his psychology was again wrong. He allowed her to see that he felt she was going to have an easy time of it when it came to getting another job. Even though he did feel that way about her, he should never have said anything. He *personalized* his feelings about her, which he should not have done. Besides that, whether or not Monica Henry could easily get a job again had nothing at all to do with the interview itself.

Even though Riley personalized during the interview, he did not actually understand Monica Henry well enough to prevent an embarrassing and unexpected development that occurred later on. He failed to do his homework on her; he did not prepare for the inevitable aftermath.

Anger and Animosity

As for the Mason interview, Riley bungled that, too, by letting his anger get the better of him. Not only did he let rage overcome him, but he insulted Mason several times. That definitely was a mistake. At the root of Riley's actions was a definite feeling of guilt, growing out of his own natural dislike of Mason.

In dealing with a subordinate whom the supervisor does not like, it is important that all discussion be restricted to the points of fact involved and not be allowed to stray. Mason's genius for ignoring the principal issue and bringing up counter issues forced

Riley to lose his cool. But Riley's inability to focus on the issues *because he had not properly studied them* was the basic reason he blew up and lost control of the dialogue.

The Keys to Termination without Guilt

The attitude with which Mark Andrews approached the termination interviews was almost the antithesis of Don Riley's. In the first place, Andrews had prepared himself extremely well for the interviews by collecting all the background material he could on his three terminatees. He knew exactly how much severance each would be getting, as noted. He also knew all about their performance records; he had them in hand, in fact.

What was most important was that Andrews was able to enter the interview phase without self-censure or guilt. Knowing that the three people had to go, he researched their backgrounds and their past efforts relentlessly until he had all the backup material he needed to convince them that they were indeed not performing up to the proper level.

Thus armed with all the facts necessary to prove the truth about the three people involved, Mark Andrews had no psychological hang-ups. He did not, for example, fear that one or two or even all three of them were getting a raw deal by being terminated. Nor did he feel that he was in any way at fault for their going. He knew that they had created their own futures and that this was simply a working out of what would be.

By preparing for their dismissals in an individualized and detailed manner, he was able to be totally impersonal when it came to the final interviews. That was the key advantage to his careful preparation.

Later on we'll study the guidelines for termination point by point. Needless to say, Don Riley's interviews were nightmares of hostility and animosity because of his lack of preparation; Mark Andrews's were effective demonstrations of empathy and dignity because of his extensive preparation.

CHAPTER 3

Considerations of Seniority

THERE ARE THREE principal criteria used by management to determine who will be terminated in a situation involving a reduction in force due to economic reasons:

- Seniority
- Performance
- Conduct

The catch phrase "due to economic reasons" means that economic conditions—either in the economy at large or within the company itself—do not warrant the company's survival with its present overhead.

Reduction in force—called "riffing," from its acronym *rif*—usually calls for a certain percentage of workers to be laid off across the board. That means that employees will be selected for riffing equally across the top (or bottom) of all departments.

Obviously, the most important criterion, and the one followed faithfully by companies throughout the country at all times in an across-the-board rif, is seniority. Performance, the next criterion used to determine who will be terminated in a reduction in force, is second to seniority in importance. If the seniority of two workers is the same, the worker whose performance is above average will be retained; the worker whose performance is below par will be let go before the more effective worker. The third criterion used to determine who will be terminated in a reduction in force, conduct that is unbecoming, might actually be called *mis*conduct rather than conduct. Obviously, misconduct is a corollary to performance that is deemed unsatisfactory.

Each of these three points is acceptable to the courts as a reason for fair dismissal in the event the termination is challenged by the employee. However, these three reasons must be documented in detail or demonstrable beyond a reasonable doubt so that the courts can decide.

Discharge "for Cause"

In spite of the overwhelming power of seniority as a yardstick to measure an employee's retainability factor, it is used only in the case of an overall reduction in staff or in the cutback of a specific department for any reason whatsoever.

In any individual case of termination, performance and conduct can offset seniority at any time. When an employer terminates an employee due to dissatisfaction, the employer is said to be discharging the employee "for cause." There are a great many different varieties of "cause." The employee may be fired for unacceptable performance, for excessive absenteeism, for unavailability, for simple inability to perform the work required, for misconduct, or for other reasons associated with these.

In case history number 1, Don Riley was forced to terminate his assistant Randy White because White was simply unable to perform the work required, due to corporate burnout. The fact that he had a great deal of seniority over many other employees at the company had nothing to do with the fact that he was selected by his supervisor to go.

It is true that Riley's reason for selecting Monica Henry for termination was partly due to the fact that she was the last person hired in the department. However, the *operative* reason she was fired was because of her inability to do the job as well as her peers. In Arthur Mason's case, Riley felt he should go because of his inability to get along well with his associates. Certainly Riley was considering his termination from a standpoint of conduct and performance and did not take seniority into account at all.

Nor was seniority any criterion in Mark Andrews's decision to terminate Jim Young in case history number 4. Mary Healy and Dick Barton also had to go for combinations of reasons involving conduct and performance, without regard to seniority.

A Typical Reduction in Force

The classic case in which seniority becomes the main factor in the selection of candidates for termination is that of a required reduction in force demanded by economic conditions. Such a rif may be necessitated by the overall economic condition of the country, by the economic state of the particular industry, or by the financial status of the company itself.

Such a reason transcends "individual rights" to employment—even those rights protected by statutes and by court precedents.

Let's take a look at a typical reduction in force and examine some of the reasons for it. Then we'll go on to take a closer look at the rules of seniority and their variations.

What are the usual reasons for an across-the-board rif?

- A company may move from one location to another by choice or due to a desire to improve quarters, unavailability of company property because of new construction, or a need to find a better pool of workers. In the case of such a move, one result is a reduction in force not only by the parent company but by the employees who do not want to go along.
- A company may close down an obsolete plant and throw all of its employees there out of work. This is riffing in its most dramatic form.
- A company may find itself obliged to cut down on its personnel because of the cancellation of a government contract on which it depends.
- A company may have to reduce its personnel simply because of changes in the sales market causing it to lose money on the particular product it makes.

- A company may go out of business because it has become obsolete and cannot compete in the current marketplace.

No matter what the reasons, the results are the same. The employer must terminate many employees. This includes not only the lower-echelon workers but middle-level managers and even top executives as well. Generally speaking, the terminated employee has little recourse to sue for reinstatement.

Mergers, acquisitions, reorganizations, changes in technology, and changes in personnel that cause interpersonal conflicts—all these can bring about a reduction in force in any company, no matter what its size.

The Rules of Seniority

Reduction in force is a problem that differs a great deal from the problem of termination for unsatisfactory performance or misconduct. Performance is an individual action; riffing is collective.

Because of that fact, the scenario for riffing in no way resembles the scenario for individual termination. In fact, most reductions in force are accomplished through an assessment of general seniority, regardless of performance or conduct.

The first consideration is the observation of "lifo." *Lifo* is an acronym for the phrase "last in first out." The newest employee is the first to go during a typical rif.

The Different Kinds of Seniority

There are several different layers involving layoff procedures, however—layers that further define seniority and point up exceptions to the rule. There are, in truth, three different kinds of seniority:

- *General seniority* means that only the employee's *time* in the job counts.

- *Secondary seniority* means that seniority determines the order of termination, assuming that all persons with the same seniority are able to perform the work.
- *Tertiary seniority* means that seniority governs dismissal only if ability and other factors are equal.

In addition to these three layers of seniority, there are two other categories:

- *Superseniority, union-type* means that certain union representatives are given a special type of seniority to protect them and to assure the union of always having a representative on the spot.
- *Superseniority, management-type* means that certain key executives are given a special type of seniority to protect them from riffing and to assure the company of their presence on the scene.

Aside from these two particular exceptions and the conditions in the three main types of seniority, most reductions in force are accomplished with a minimum of hassle because most employees generally agree to abide by seniority rules. When seniority rules and civil rights statutes collide, however, it is always the civil rights provisions that win in the courts.

CHAPTER 4

Considerations of Performance

THE MOST IMPORTANT criterion for judging a worker's worth is job performance. Usually an employee's abilities and skills speak for themselves. Co-workers know that the employee is capable of good work; his or her superiors also know it. Management, unfortunately, is not always quite so aware as it should be.

There seems little doubt that the excellence of an outstanding worker is noted by peers and superiors alike. For the average worker—the one performing at neither a superior nor an inferior level—it sometimes becomes difficult for management to evaluate effectiveness properly.

Accurate determination of a worker's good qualities and bad points is essential in correctly carrying out promotion, demotion, transfer, and termination procedures. The key word in the judgment of an employee's worth, not only by peers but by management, is *fairness*. A good worker may become involved in a situation in which his or her abilities are ignored, and certain extraneous factors can contribute to make the worker *look* bad, thus precipitating reprimands from management. This can cause a decline in morale in any company.

For this reason, most companies maintain performance charts on every employee—from line workers to top management—in order to appraise each employee's skills and defects on a continuing basis. Evaluation procedures are used not only to select managers for promotion or salary increase but also to motivate workers on all levels to improve their performance.

The purpose of an honest evaluation program is to give each

49

worker a fair shake. With the criteria of evaluation applied objectively and consistently, management can get a good picture of every one of its workers. The superior performer becomes recognized as such; the inferior performer and the troublemaker become isolated as well. Honest evaluation prevents favoritism and bias in promotions, transfers, and terminations.

But evaluation is even more important from a standpoint of legal action. A good evaluation procedure is a must in any company—large or small. It is the key to maintaining documentation and to collecting specific information to allay charges of discrimination in termination actions.

With a good rating system, management can determine who should be promoted, who should be given further training, and who is not a likely prospect for a more difficult job. There have been a number of significant changes in rating systems through the years. Many early examples of evaluation procedures emphasized personality traits and such rather subjective assessments as psychological profiles as well as such difficult-to-ascertain valuations as "results" measured against preset goals and objectives.

Is There a Perfect Evaluation Program?

No perfect evaluation system really exists. However, by balancing several different assessments made by various individuals, management can secure some kind of relatively accurate performance estimate.

Evaluation forms are changing even now. The typical conventional performance rating is generally in the form of a series of statements with appropriate numbers following the statements—usually a range of five different assessments (reminiscent of grades A through F used in educational ratings): exceptional, very good, good, fair, unsatisfactory.

In addition to the series of assessments of traits and abilities, the form usually contains several specific questions to which the evaluator responds using his or her own judgment to point out defects to be corrected and explain how they might be improved, along with a fairly long subjective comment on the employee.

The Trait-Rating Evaluation Method

A typical series of trait-rating evaluation items looks like this:

Job knowledge: Theoretical and practical know-how in present job.

Attitude: Enthusiasm for job. Loyalty to company. Ability to accept criticism.

Creativity: Ability to develop new plans, cut costs, improve efficiency.

Leadership: Ability to motivate subordinates to better work effort.

Judgment: Ability to analyze facts and apply sound judgment to the work problem.

Personal efficiency: Speed and effectiveess in carrying out duties.

Dependability: Reliability in carrying out assignments conscientiously.

Interpersonal relations: Ability to deal with other people. Tact. Diplomacy. Authority.

Delegation: Ability to assign work to others and coordinate workload.

Each of these items is graded from 1 through 5, with the lower score on the negative side (1 = unsatisfactory; 5 = exceptional). Each of these grades is then tallied in a final computation to determine the individual's total score. Obviously the employee with the highest score is the most able worker.

After the series of graded items comes another section involving a question or series of questions like the following:

Note three performance characteristics of the employee that need improvement.

What might the employee do to improve job performance? Are there any health or personal problems that might be affecting the employee's work performance? Comments?

The type of form described is called a "graphic rating" or a "rating score." It is obvious that the numerical score is not going to evaluate all people effectively. For example, a person with exceptional creativity (a Thomas A. Edison, for example), even though scoring 5 in creativity, might score very low on almost every other item.

In effect, such an evaluation procedure buries a highly creative individual and makes him or her look totally ineffective. The same is true of a person with exceptional interpersonal relations potential who knows little and cares less about specific job functions.

Specifically, the trait-rating evaluation tends to give a special advantage to the conformist, the person who hides in the middle but never tries to do anything exceptionally good *or* bad. Another problem involving trait-rating evaluation is that it puts little emphasis on measurable job performance.

Other Rating Methods

To try to overcome the limitations of the traditional evaluation form, several new types of measurements have been devised, including:

- Forced distribution
- Forced choice
- Critical incident

Forced Distribution

Forced distribution is simply an attempt to rank employees by class, or ability, in five different categories: highest class (10 percent) second class (20 percent), third class (40 percent), fourth class (20 percent), lowest class (10 percent). To anyone who has graded a class of students on a curve, there is an obvious similarity between a typical A to F curve and this method of forced distribution.

The system does prevent overleniency in evaluating employees. However, it has one primary drawback. It assumes that all groups contain the same proportion of outstanding, average, and poor employees. This is simply not true, particularly where there are only a few employees in a given group.

Forced Choice

Forced choice is the professional psychologist's attempt to free evaluation programs from typical favoritism or prejudice. It attempts to rate an employee by comparing two apparently favorable and two apparently unfavorable traits, applying two out of four choices to the individual. The evaluator reads four statements about a particular trait, then checks one as the *least* characteristic of the person and another as the *most* characteristic. For example:

	MOST	LEAST
Knows capabilities and limitations of employees.	_____	_____
Doesn't usually pull rank.	_____	_____
Has no control over employees.	_____	_____
Never loses temper.	_____	_____

There are obviously two positive factors and two negative factors in the four statements. However, only one of the positive factors counts; the second positive rates zero in the scoring. The positive that counts is the first statement: "Knows capabilities and limitations of employees." The negative that counts is the third statement: "Has no control over employees." The positive that doesn't count and the negative that doesn't count are the two remaining statements.

In developing such a test, psychologists feel that only by being tricked into making a correct decision can the evaluator come up with a truly objective and accurate answer. But of course, any evaluator worth his or her salt will try to figure out what the psychologists had in mind to begin with.

Forced choice is resented by evaluators who are trying to do an honest appraisal of their subordinates. One says: "I don't know what those psychologists are trying to do. I don't know what answer they want. I try to reward my good employees by giving them good ratings—but I can't even be sure I'm doing that!" Another points out that psychological tricks should not be part of a good evaluation system. "We think our own judgment is better."

Critical Incident

The critical incident method involves a system of selective job requirements, such as "developing new customers" for a sales manager or "avoiding losses" for a marketing manager. Once the performance record program has been drawn up for each job, the manager is on the lookout for "critical incidents," or outstanding examples of success or failure in meeting the requirements. For example:

September 30.   Shipment of valves late at railhead.
December 15.   Signed up Smith, Inc., for supplies.
March 10.   Production three days behind schedule.

Although the system tends to be hit-and-miss, it is based on objective evidence rather than on a more subjective assessment of personality traits. It is not a matter of pointing out that a particular employee cannot deal with people; the supervisor must cite specific instances of the employee's inability to do so.

The Evaluation Interview

One the evaluation has been made—with one form of the preceding methods or with a combination of various forms—the supervisor or evaluator sits down with the employee to discuss the findings.

Many managers find the evaluation interview distasteful. They hate to tell an employee about deficiencies. In their aversion to telling the employee that he or she is not doing well, many hide behind a facade of self-deception by feeling that all the employees know how they are doing through some imagined company grapevine. But in some instances, the evaluation interview is the only one-on-one chance management has to point out to its workers that they may not be performing up to par.

A typical evaluation interview usually breaks down into the following five parts:

- Purpose
- Evaluation rundown
- Feedback
- Problem solving
- Goals and objectives

Purpose

In discussing the purpose of the interview, the evaluator explains that the entire evaluation program is set up in order to help the employee do a better job. The point is made that without occasional evaluation information, the employee might not know that he or she is making mistakes. The object of it all is to improve job performance.

Evaluation Rundown

The evaluator then goes over the evaluation sheet point by point, starting with the strong points first (the positive side) and then the weak points (the negative side). It is inadvisable for the evaluator to hand the evaluation sheet or sheets to the employee for firsthand perusal. The evaluator picks out the salient points for discussion ahead of time and then goes over them one by one in detail.

An employee is not entitled to see *all* the information on file. Some of it may be confidential material that management wants to withhold. For example, there might be notes about a discussion of a chance for promotion that was not given or a supervisor's personal reaction to a request the employee brought in for consideration. This confidential material might also include data from fellow workers that have been noted as private and not for the subject to view. Nor does the evaluator have to be completely frank about the employee's prospects in the company, either. Prospects have a way of changing from one day to the next; it is neither fair nor intelligent to reveal such data that might be out of date when seen by the employee.

Feedback

The employee is invited to give his or her own comments about job performance, particularly those selected for mention in the evaluation. The evaluator must anticipate some hostility or anger in this response, particularly if the evaluation has been largely a negative one. The purpose of this stage of the interview is to let the employee blow off a little steam, if necessary. The evaluator usually takes the position that while there may be extenuating circumstances, these should not be used to completely negate the evaluator's charges.

Problem Solving

The interview now enters the problem-solving stage, in which the evaluator encourages the employee to give his or her side of the situation, to elaborate in detail on feedback already noted. The employee is invited to stress the problems that are being solved, anticipate other problems that are coming up and must be resolved, and present his or her general picture of the situation.

Goals and Objectives

The evaluator ends the discussion by telling the employee what can be done to overcome all weak points and what management can do to try to help the employee over the rough spots. The evaluator absorbs any criticism or aggression from the employee, holding argument in abeyance and never bothering to contradict. The purpose of this phase of the interview is to allow the employee to save a little face by not exposing the falsity of unjustified alibis and promises. The meeting can end on a note of confidence, with goals and objectives spelled out for the future.

Note: A classic example of the wrong kind of evaluation technique starts with the evaluator asking the employee, "How do *you* think you're doing?" and then letting the employee carry the ball for the first segment of the interview. Then the evaluator hands the employee the evaluation form to see how close the guess has been. The problem with this system is that it reeks of gamesmanship. The employee *knows* an evaluation will be reviewed. The question becomes one of how much weakness should be admitted to. How much does the boss want to hear? What does the boss really know? And so on. For this reason, it is wise to avoid this type of approach.

The Importance of Evaluation in Termination

The point is: What has evaluation to do with termination? In many cases, even if the employee's evaluation is bad, he or she may never be fired. In other cases, even if an employee's evaluation is good, he or she may not last another month in the job anyway.

Nevertheless, as unconnected with termination as evaluation may seem to be, there is a definite tie-in. Particularly in the area of "fairness," the evaluation itself can prove to be invaluable.

If the employee knows of shortcomings, the act of termination may not seem so sudden and surprising, even though it will still be traumatic. Properly performed evaluation procedures and properly conducted interviews contribute to an important backlog of documentation demonstrating the company's interest in and regard for the employee's situation.

Management's understanding of the employee's abilities and shortcomings leads to a much greater confidence that there *is* an element of fairness and equity in hiring, in promoting, in demoting, in transferring, and even in terminating.

Fairness in termination neutralizes a great deal of anger, despair, and outright hostility in the employee. It also neutralizes the same rage and hostility in the entire work force—rage and hostility that, unchecked, can contribute to a dramatic drop in morale.

From the standpoint of management, of course, the real value of proper evaluation is its inherent protection of the company against lawsuits challenging the termination of an employee for unsatisfactory performance. The employee's suit is usually based on demonstrating that he or she was never reprimanded for performing in an inferior manner.

Evaluation documents, when correctly and honestly filled out, can refute such a claim.

What the Courts Require

In trying a case against an employer for "unfair" termination for unsatisfactory performance, a court usually looks long and hard at the appraisal program that has produced the performance records—assuming, of course, that such documentation exists.

There are three criteria by which a court evaluates an appraisal program:

- It must be justifiable.
- It must be relevant.
- It must be reliable.

Justifiability

The evaluation program must be fully accepted and understood by both management and the work force. It must be demonstrably useful, necessary, and objective. The program must be shown to be able to rate individual performance fairly and accurately. The purpose of the evaluation process must be clearly stated, and the procedures must be clear and uncluttered with vague generalities.

Employees as well as management must be able to participate in the program's ongoing process. Both must also have had a hand in designing its methodology. The whole point of the program must be to fulfill the program's purposes.

Relevancy

The evaluation program must make clear statements of job requirements and job activities, along with attitude and behavior expected of workers for successful performance of duties. A relevant program should not rely on personality quirks, racial prejudices, sexual biases, or considerations of age.

It should focus instead on the ability and skills of the employees and examine in detail how each employee goes about his or her work. It should also be able to evaluate the nature of the output and results of each employee's work habits.

In effect, the program should concentrate on important aspects of work only, not on minor details and irrelevant considerations.

Reliability

The evaluation program should be consistent—that is, evaluation sheets should be documented regularly on either an annual or a semiannual basis. The evaluations themselves must be consistent, in spite of the fact that various records will have been filled out by different people.

Each evaluation should be prepared with a minimum of subjective determination and a maximum of objective reasoning. The evaluator must be prevented from distorting the appraisals. A good program should allow the evaluator to measure the output of each employee in units of productivity.

If only indirect measures can be used, these should be scaled to compare accurately with direct measures. The evaluator should assess the ability of the appraisal system in advance, making sure it uses consistent and honest standards of measurement.

In a good evaluation program, if the scales of measurement

are 1 to 5, each point should be anchored to reality by specific descriptions available at all times to anyone studying the evaluation sheets.

Guidelines for an Ideal Evaluation Program

The following is a set of guidelines to be used to upgrade an evaluation program to a level where the courts will judge it successful:

- *The program should apply specific performance standards to each employee's work.* In other words, the courts want to see job performance standards based on empirical, demonstrable analysis, including interviews, questionnaires, observations, and other work analyses providing documented data.
- *The program should be rationally designed.* The process should be clear and reasonable, with each step properly identified. The techniques adopted in achieving an effective evaluation process should be stated as objectives for the program.
- *The program should document performance evaluations.* A hit-and-miss approach to evaluation is no good in court. There should be an obviously equitable treatment of all groups of employees. There should also be a concern for regular, recurring appraisals as a matter of routine. Systematic procedures and policies of administration should be evident, too.
- *The program should administer the rating systematically.* Evaluation should be done at least once a year, possibly twice a year. Each evaluation sheet should be filed away and kept for reference for at least three years.
- *The company should train all evaluators and monitor their work consistently.* Each evaluator should be able to rate each employee accurately within the parameters of the system set up by the evaluation program. Each evaluator should also have input into the system and be allowed to suggest changes in the system at any time.

How an Evaluation Program Pays Off

The effectiveness of a good evaluation program in a termination action can be seen by comparing the exit interviews of Don Riley and Mark Andrews. In case histories number 5 and number 6—those of Dick Barton and Mary Healy—Mark Andrews had, as usual, done his homework efficiently. Not only had he maintained proper evaluation charts on the two of them, but he also had copies of the charts with him at the termination interviews.

As a matter of fact, he even cited Healy's low scoring on attitude, personal efficiency, interpersonal relations and dependability—all of which she was weak in. Such a background of opinion, documented and filed, was effectively marshaled against her if she were to try to challenge Andrews's termination.

With Barton, Andrews simply cited his overall low scores on the charts—which really showed nothing of the incident that had led to his dismissal.

If Don Riley, in case history number 3—that of Monica Henry—had been able to present an evaluation chart later on in court to show that her performance as a secretary had been judged to be poor by her superiors, he would not have had the trouble he did in trying to prove that he had fired her for her inability to perform. (We shall see what happened in the Monica Henry case in chapter 9.)

The same is true of Arthur Mason, case history number 2, whose evaluation chart might very well have shown him to be unable to get along with his fellow workers—had one been kept. The company's lack of evaluation charts left management wide open when it came to Henry's and Mason's lawsuits—as we shall see.

CHAPTER 5

Considerations of Behavior

STATISTICS SHOW that the most common reason for discharge of an employee for unsatisfactory performance on the job is absenteeism, sometimes called "unavailability" in personnel jargon. Termination for absenteeism can be adjudged either a form of unsatisfactory performance or a form of misconduct.

Misconduct usually refers to pilfering on the job, fighting in the work area, or breaking the rules and regulations of the company. Nevertheless, it can also refer to absenteeism as a form of conduct unbecoming an employee.

Even misconduct must be carefully studied by management before being applied as a measure of performance to justify termination. If a claim of misconduct can be proved to serve as a shield for discrimination—because of sex, race, age, religion, or handicap—the courts will come out against management and for the employee.

Termination with Awareness

A hastily decided termination based on emotional considerations or personal animosity can not only bring about a problem in company morale but may also lead to all kinds of legal complications if the action violates any of the statutory provisions covering protected groups of employees or goes against any of the recent court precedents regarding "public policy" and "fairness."

Today, more than ever before, the decision to terminate must be made with a clear head and an awareness of the problems involving not only potential lawsuits but the morale of the organization itself. Fairness and justice have become an obsession with employees on all levels.

The complications that may arise from charges of discrimination are reserved for a later chapter; this chapter is confined to problems that might result from firing for disciplinary infractions.

It goes without saying today that a decision to terminate an employee for misconduct must be free of any demonstrable evidence of bias, subjectivity, or malicious intent. Otherwise, the organization may find itself the target of court action or government agency pressure.

Viewing the problem from the standpoint of management, there are a number of important factors that must be considered before a fully informed decision can be made. At least three of these factors must be thoroughly covered:

- Investigation of all the facts.
- Uniform enforcement and administration of regulations.
- Documentation of details.

In any case of termination—for dishonesty, for direct disobedience, for immoral conduct—the employer must make sure that the person or persons selected for termination are not being chosen out of malice, out of ignorance of the true facts, or out of personal bias.

If the facts leading up to the termination are correctly identified, if there is uniform enforcement of discipline, and if documentation of the case is accurate, management cannot be accused of "unfairness," "injustice," "wrongful discharge," or "indiscriminate behavior."

Investigation of the Facts

The only way a supervisor can confidently and honestly terminate an employee for misconduct is by examining all the possible complications that might have caused the employee to perform below expectations, defy superiors, or otherwise fail in the job. In some cases, job qualifications become shifted around when a company strives to keep up with the competition; a worker who was qualified when hired eventually becomes unqualified. If a new manager comes in and fires this employee, the morale of the other workers plummets.

Supervisors and managers must keep up with the twists and turns that occur in every corner of their departments and divisions. Only by keeping accurate evaluation sheets, as discussed in the preceding chapter, and by investigating activity on all levels can management be confident that it knows who is performing above average and who below.

Once a thorough investigation has been made, giving the employee's views and arguments as well as those of his or her supervisor objective study and consideration, then management will be able to effect a termination without fear of retaliation. It is the only way to prevent arbitrary decisions and personally motivated moves that can cause time-wasting and money-wasting upheavals.

Uniform Enforcement of Regulations

All companies have rules and regulations regarding behavior, whether they are written and posted or simply implied and tacitly understood. Such a code of behavior involves an entire range of behavioral matters, including holiday and vacation schedules, safety rules, work breaks, lunch hours, private telephone calls, dress codes (if any), and drinking on the premises.

It is up to management to enforce these rules and regulations in an unbiased and uniform manner. If any employee is allowed to get away with an infraction, no matter how small, other employees will resent it. On the other hand, if the infraction is picayune, immediate and stern enforcement sometimes causes as much resentment in the other direction. In both cases, the effect on the rest of the company can be a drop in morale.

Punishment for an infraction must be not only uniform but immediate. A long lapse between the time of an infraction and punishment for the infraction can lead first to a drop in morale and then to irritation on the part of the perpetrator at being made to do penance for an act that occurred in the dim past!

All punishment must be objective. Once the individual who has transgressed pays for the transgression—whether by suspension from work, by extra hours, or by withholding of pay—the infraction has been paid for and is no longer held against the employee.

Note: Although a transgressor is allowed to feel that his or her misstep has been paid for, it must always be noted on the records. One misstep followed by a clean record is one thing; one misstep followed by a second misstep followed by a third is another thing. For the first-time offender, correction of the error is enough. For the third-time offender, the record speaks for itself.

Detailed Documentation of Facts

Both the investigation of facts and the enforcement of regulations must be fully documented in the personnel file of the individual employee. The investigation of facts in an argument between two employees about a particular action, for example, should be written up as a record of the event. This record must be maintained in the files of both employees. If the investigation leads to the punishment of one of the employees—or both—the punishment must also be detailed, in writing, and preserved.

Documentation is extremely important in maintaining an objective and unbiased attitude. The memorandum or report of a violation of regulations must not be hidden from other employees. While it is not necessary to post it to humiliate the transgressor, it is a good idea for it to be available for study by anyone who might be interested.

Such a paper trail is particularly important if an infraction should become the basis of a dismissal that is subsequently challenged either by an unemployment referee, a fair employment practices investigator, an arbitrator, or a court. Documentation of each move made is the best way for the employer to prove impartiality in dealing with the employee who has been terminated for misconduct. The documentation shows that for each step taken, there was adequate and impartial investigation, adjugment, and decision.

Even though documentation may seem to be a waste of time, it is the easiest way to protect the company against a charge of inequity of action. It also assures all the company's employees that judgments are objective and impartial. To the outside world, documentation shows that:

1. The employee involved was warned about the first minor offense.
2. The employee continued with repeated offenses or inferior performance.
3. All employees were aware of the policy or issue involved in the infractions.
4. The termination decision was justified and appropriate after all the facts were weighed.

Obviously, a termination decision that has been uniformly approached from the beginning, is based on proof of misconduct, and has been adequately documented will be easier and less costly to justify and defend than one that has not.

Progressive Discipline and How It Works

For discipline to be fairly administered and uniformly applied, and for a termination procedure to be just and fair, a system of progressive discipline must be in force. *Progressive discipline* is a term used to describe a series of rules and regulations involving steps to take to prevent or punish infractions of rules and regulations.

No one disciplinary system is universal; every company, big or small, has a different type. Some companies have different rules and regulations for different strata of employees. This is legitimate from a legal standpoint, providing the employees in each stratum are treated equally and uniformly. But generally, most corporations like their rules and regulations to apply with equal force to everyone. Justice has been pictured as being blind. Such impartiality should exist in corporate situations as well as everywhere else.

There are five steps in a system of progressive discipline:

1. Counseling
2. Written reprimands.
3. Appeals
4. Final warning
5. Termination

For each reprimand there is a possible appeal. Steps two and three can occur three to five times; usually the maximum limit on appeals is three. A time limit should be set within which the employee's performance is given a chance to improve.

Step 1: Counseling

When an employee steps out of line and breaks a company's rule or regulation, he or she should be called in by a superior and informed of the misstep. It is at this meeting that the superior should counsel the employee in an effort to avoid a repetition of the mistake in the future.

In an ideal situation, the supervisor should make a maximum effort to point out to the employee exactly what went wrong and instruct him or her on how to avoid a repetition.

Counseling should take place at the time the employee is informed of the infraction. If the discussion is postponed, the employee will think that nothing really wrong was done.

In most cases, a single session of counseling with a supervisor will be enough to solve the problem and make further action unnecessary. Such a counseling session should be documented in memo form and the memo inserted in the employee's file.

Step 2: Written Reprimand

If, after the first step of informing the employee of the mistake and counseling him or her on better procedure, the infraction recurs, the supervisor should inform the employee in writing of the repetition of the original infraction. In this written memorandum, the employer should point out that the employee has already been counseled about the mistake but has failed to heed the warning.

In addition, the reprimand should emphasize the importance

of the situation, clearly describing the infraction and reviewing the previous discussion of the subject. In the reprimand the supervisor should clearly define the standards of performance expected. A time limit should also be set, by which date the employee must have corrected the error, or the performance shortcoming.

The reprimand should also contain a clear assessment of the consequences of the employee's continued failure to perform the job satisfactorily. This should include such warning consequences as lack of promotion, deferral of salary increase, and even possible loss of job.

One copy of a typical reprimand should go to the employee. A second copy should go in his or her personnel file. A third should be kept in the supervisor's file, with a follow-up date noted on it to remind the supervisor to check the employee's progress.

If the employee does improve, a note should be made of that fact and the memorandum placed in the employee's personnel file.

Step 3: Appeal

Almost every large company has some kind of procedure set up by which an employee may appeal a reprimand or a dismissal. Such a channel should be kept open at all times. Not every supervisor is objective; sometimes emotions cloud the mind and make rulings subjective instead.

At each step of the progressive discipline system, there should be an escape hatch for the employee by means of which he or she can appeal to a higher authority to make sure the reprimand or warning is in fact objective and "fair." In an ideal situation, there should be provision for an appeal after each reprimand.

Step 4: Final Warning

After a specified number of reprimands—usually no more than three—the supervisor should write out a final warning to the employee, stating that if the infraction or performance shortcoming is not corrected, the employee will be terminated for cause.

The point of the final warning is that the responsibility for any such termination lies completely in the hands of the employee. It should be stressed that he or she has been warned time and again about bringing performance up to standard but has failed to do so.

The final warning should contain the following:

- A copy of the memorandum of the original counseling session.
- Copies of all previous reprimands.
- A list of particular performance shortcomings that must be improved.
- A specific period of time that is being allowed for correction of unsatisfactory performance.
- A statement that the employee has one more chance to bring his or her performance level up to standard, within the set time limit, or face termination.
- A copy of the warning for the employee.
- A copy of the warning for his or her personnel file.
- A copy of the warning for the supervisor's file.

If the employee improves to such an extent that he or she corrects whatever made performance unsatisfactory, the supervisor should prepare a memorandum to the effect that the employee is removed from the status of final warning and will remain free so long as satisfactory performance is maintained. A copy of this should be given to the employee, with a copy for the personnel file and a copy for the supervisor's file.

If the unsatisfactory performance then recurs, the supervisor can reinstate the final warning.

Step 5: Dismissal

Once the supervisor decides that the employee has not been able to correct the shortcomings that led to the first reprimand, he or she should make sure that the employee is fully aware of the reprimands and the final warning and that the employee knows he or she may be terminated if the stated obligations are not fulfilled.

When all these steps are covered, and the supervisor is sure that the documents are on file and that the employee is fully warned, he or she should inform the employee of the termination action.

Usually an employee is awarded a certain amount of severance pay upon termination. The amount awarded may be spelled out in company policy, or it may be negotiable. A typical severance package is examined in chapters two and ten.

The employee should be informed that the severance pay is independent of his or her work at the company and is neither earned money nor money accrued during employment. It is a separate package to provide economic support during the period when he or she is out of work and looking for another job.

How Important Documentation Can Be

When Mark Andrews terminated Mary Healy in case history number 6, he pointed out to her that she had exhausted every possible measure in the company's appeal procedure. During the termination interview, he had copies of all her records in hand to quote to her if necessary. In the event that she might decide to sue in the courts for reinstatement, he had prepared the company's case as carefully as possible. So had he for the terminations of Jim Young and Dick Barton.

However, when Don Riled terminated Randy White in case history number 1, he did not have any documentation on White's failures as assistant marketing director. In fact, he had nothing in hand to prove that White was performing inadequately. One of Riley's problems was that the company itself had no appeals setup. For that reason, the termination was missing a vital ingredient: documentation to offset a challenge from White in the event that he decided to sue for reinstatement—which, in fact, he did.

As for Riley's dismissal of Monica Henry in case history number 3, he had nothing to show in support of his assessment of her lack of ability to perform her job. Had he prepared a step-by-step memo of verbal reprimands from any source whatsoever, had he even included statements from various managers as to her slowness or poor performance rating, he would have been on more solid ground. Riley's preparation for the dismissal of Monica Henry was abysmally inadequate from its inception to its conclusion.

Again, in the case of Arthur Mason, Riley had come to the termination interview woefully unprepared. He had completely forgotten about Mason's criticism of the company's airplane valve, and he had no concrete proof of Mason's supposed altercations with other employees. Nor did he have any evaluation or discipline records to prove that Mason was performing unsatisfactorily. Any case against Mason was at best ephemeral.

Fairness and Justice

Today the supervisor must realize that he or she is working in a world that did not exist several decades ago. The termination at will concept is still alive, but it is ailing. Reduction in force, unfit performance, misconduct—all are valid reasons for dismissal. Yet even these reasons must be spelled out and made clear to the employee to abrogate the possibility of a lawsuit charging discrimination or unfairness.

Fairness does not mean, literally, "justice." Fairness means that a termination has been handled objectively, in an equitable manner, so that one "victim" is not singled out to be punished for what other employees have done.

The court system looks favorably on fairness in the current sociological climate. The burden is now on the employer to prove fairness in any dismissal. The employee can simply cry "foul," and the employer must take action to prove that no foul occurred.

Proof of fairness lies in good rapport between employer and employee, clarity of communication between the two, concise reports, documented evidence of unsatisfactory performance, proof of sufficient warning of dismissal, and evidence of empathy and compassion in the employer's attempts to help the employee—even though the situation has ended in termination.

CHAPTER 6

Alternatives to Dismissal

To NOTE AN employee's failure to perform adequately in a job and then initiate termination procedures immediately is a crass and undignified way for any corporation to behave—especially one concerned with its image of compassion and humanity.

At the very first indication of an employee's failure to perform or of an employee's deliberate disregard of rules and regulations, a superior should intervene to try to find out what is causing these shortcomings.

The first and most effective method of trying to deal with such a sudden change in performance is for the worker's immediate supervisor to approach him or her to try to find out its cause. Take the case of Jim Neal's supervisor, who reported the following:

> I always thought of Jim Neal as a typically no-nonsense line worker. He never had any weird hang-ups like some of the others. Yet in June, very suddenly, he began clocking in one or two hours late. His work on the line got sloppy. Although his co-workers covered for him, I learned that he had caused about a thousand dollar's worth of repairs on his machine—just by carelessness.
>
> I finally got him into the office and tried to find out what was bothering him. His wife had walked out, he told me. She was living with another man. She was trying to make their only child—a twelve-year-old boy—join her and her live-in lover.
>
> That would be enough to drive any human being up the wall, so I got Jim some therapy and a lawyer. Both helped. He finally

got a divorce and gained custody of his boy. And his job performance improved dramatically so that he was his old self again.

Not all worker shortcomings are caused by a single, specific problem, such as the marital relationship cited above. Frequently, the problems are much more complicated and difficult to detect. The point is, at the very first indication of deterioration in a worker's performance, his or her superior should make a note of it immediately and try to find out what is causing it.

Although many large corporations have effective employee review procedures, probably the majority do not. Many executives feel that what they don't know won't hurt them—particularly in regard to their immediate subordinates' life-styles, emotional situations, or personal hang-ups.

A review program differs from a grievance program in that the review process is always initiated by management, not by the workers. Review can be an adjunct to evaluation but is not nearly so formal, specific, or work-related.

The purpose of a review program is to isolate, identify, and diagnose emotional, psychological, and personal problems that might affect a worker's performance. It is, in a sense, preventive medicine rather than curative medicine.

In some instances a review program can spot a problem in an employee's working situation before it becomes so uncontrollable as to endanger the worker's performance or his or her feeling of confidence and self-assurance.

For example, if it is functioning effectively, the program can determine an employee's ineptitude with respect to an assigned work area that might not have been evident from an original aptitude test or personnel interview. The obvious solution for such a problem is to shift the worker to another area before instituting reprimands under the progressive discipline system.

If, on the other hand, it is the worker who is deteriorating on the job for some internal reason, that, too, can be detected in time, as in the case of the worker whose wife had left him and was trying to take their child with her.

Reviewing employees from the standpoint of mental and physical health can prevent the possibility of termination from arising in the first place, and it can also clarify alternatives to dismissal at the point of termination. Such a system can be set up with a few guidelines in mind, as discussed in the next section.

Guidelines for a Good Review System

An effective review system contains the following elements:

- Promptness
- Informality
- Consistency
- Accessibility
- Explanation
- Justification
- Correctability

Promptness of Investigation

As soon as a supervisor discovers any flaw in an employee's work, he or she should immediately try to determine what is troubling that person. A quick fix is usually not in the cards. The employee *may* tell all immediately, but generally this is not the case.

The supervisor is frequently forced to do some investigation on his or her own, discussing the situation with co-workers, going behind the scenes where possible to determine the truth. This occurs not only in cases of flaws in performance but also in personal confrontations between workers.

Eventually the supervisor should sit down with the worker and get it all out in the open. With proper investigation, enough facts can usually be gleaned for the situation to be clarified. Such an investigation must be performed quickly and without hesitation. If trouble is brewing, the employee may well be on his or her way to an attorney's office by the time a slow management isolates the problem.

Informality of Discussion

Nothing is worse than for management to adopt the attitude of the Grand Inquisitor. Any discussion with an employee must be handled in as informal and as nonthreatening a manner as possible. In the review procedure the employer should always approach the employee face-to-face rather than via paper.

At this point, the review procedure is quite similar in tone to the first step in the progressive discipline system described in the preceding chapter. In many instances, this interview may be part of both programs.

It is advisable not to employ any writing at all during this informal discussion. Rapid note taking or the humming menace of a tape recorder is very upsetting to the employee. The gist of the dialogue should be to express management's desire to help the employee out of his or her particular trouble. When an employee clams up for any reason, it is best to accept the lack of response and try again later. Coercing cooperation or revelation is nonproductive if not counterproductive.

Consistency in Management

A common complaint by employees is that the treatment of workers is not consistent. That is, one employee is required to do something that another employee working nearby or perhaps in the same job does not have to do.

One of the first things a supervisor embarking on a review investigation should check is such consistency in management procedures. It frequently happens that managers of different departments have different ideas about company policy. The investigator must first learn what company policy is and then trace it through to see where it is not being observed with the proper fidelity.

If it is a problem of consistency, the discrepancy should be noted, the guilty manager informed, and corrective measures taken.

Accessibility of the Grievance System

Although many companies have grievance systems set up for nonunion employees of all grades, one of the main problems in today's corporate world is the reluctance of many employees to use the system. Some feel that it is just a facade to make management look good.

In the case of an employee's attempt to criticize the way the company is run, some supervisors tend to be tight-lipped and unavailable. Supervisors must make themselves accessible at all times to those under them. They should also consider themselves accountable to their employees when the employees wish to see them. They should try to get employees to use the grievance system to explain their problems before they have a chance of worsening.

Explanation of the Decision

As soon as the investigative review has uncovered the facts and determined the cause of a problem, the worker involved should immediately be informed, and as soon as a decision has been made about the problem, the worker should know what has been decided.

The decision should be explained by the supervisor in easy-to-understand terms, with nothing implied or hidden from view. The explanation must be crystal-clear, comprehensible, and logical. It is useless to try to confuse and manipulate an employee by some slick, equivocal interpretation that tries to make what is bad seem good or vice versa.

Justification of Any Mistake

If management is found to be wrong in any investigation situation, the supervisor must make sure that the mistake is corrected. The fact that the problem has been corrected should immediately be communicated to the employee who reported it.

The fact should also be communicated to the entire staff so that other employees can see that the review program does work when grievances are taken to management.

Correctability of Management

If the review process has uncovered a flaw in the management system—no matter how small or how inconsequential in relation to the big picture—*it must be corrected.* One of the most important elements of a review procedure is the question management must ask itself: *Was management's claim justified?*

If it was, why did the employee not understand the situation correctly? Was the flaw in the employee or in the system?

Every case investigated in a review system must be brought up in the higher echelons of management for discussion. If there is an internal conflict, changes must be made to resolve that conflict. The conditions that caused the conflict must also be resolved so they do not reappear.

If possible, it is always best for employer and employee to confront each other face to face to discuss problems openly. Through discussion, misunderstandings can be resolved. The worker's abilities must be equal to the demands of the job. If they are not, a shift in position can easily prevent a situation in which termination is the only possible answer.

The Alternatives

Transferring an employee to another job if his or her qualifications prove to be unequal to the assigned work is the most common method of avoiding an unwanted termination. Such a condition may result when the job itself changes and adds requirements a worker cannot satisfy.

We have already seen such a situation in case history number 4, when Jim Young was terminated because the job had simply grown beyond his capabilities. Let's back up a moment and reconsider the case and the way Young's superior, Mark Andrews, actually approached the problem of Young's growing inability to perform.

Young had simply become incapable of overseeing the manufacturing division of Maddon, Inc., which had been falling seriously behind in production after Maddon bought and merged with Sylvester. The problem Andrews faced was in doing something about Young. And because of the nature of the situation, he had to do it quickly.

Andrews had a number of options open to him, such as the following:

- One option was to provide strong staff support to Young; that is, hire a group of qualified young production people to do the hands-on work for Young so he could simply manage.
- Another option was to create a special job for Young—something that had nothing to do with production except in an indirect way.
- A third option was to hire a top-notch production manager and put him or her in just over Young's head but let Young keep his title.
- A fourth option was to send Young to a training program to learn managerial skills.
- A fifth option was to demote Young to a lower level of management more suitable to his talents.
- A sixth option was to let him retain his present position and title as vice-president but, remove all real authority from him and give it to a new vice-president.
- The seventh option was to terminate him and hire someone in his place or phase out his position.

Andrews had agonized over the problem for days.

- The first option was not practical in a company the size of the Maddon operation, although it would have been a feasible alternative for a larger company. Andrews knew he couldn't hire a group to help Young.
- The second option was out, too; Andrews would need a director of manufacturing, and the "special job" ploy would be obvious.
- The third option meant spending a great deal of money to add unnecessary staff support.
- The fourth option was not feasible in Young's particular case. He was really too old to pick up any new ways of working. Besides, it would take too much time. Andrews needed quick results.
- As for the fifth option, Andrews knew that if he kept Young at his old salary in a demoted position, there would be a long-term morale problem. The rest of his employees would be angry at this example of favoritism.
- The sixth option was no good, either. The move would demoralize Young, perhaps forcing him to resign, which would be bad for the company's image.
- The seventh option was the only one possible.

In another situation, a superior faced with a problem similar to Andrews's might have been able to choose option six: keep Young in his present position and give all his authority to a new vice-president. However, Andrews was unable to do so and was now faced with a termination situation.

Termination is a last-resort option, of course. In the case of Jim Young, termination was the only way to go. And Young was a special case, being very high in the managerial echelon with little leeway for movement up or down—or even sideways.

For the average employee, in contrast, there are usually about four general options that management can take advantage of:

• Early retirement
• Bumping
• Attrition
• Buyout

Early Retirement

In the case of an older worker, an employer can sometimes make a termination resemble a voluntary early retirement. If it can be effected in that manner, it is a welcome alternative to outright termination or forced retirement.

A recent corporate survey has shown that almost two-thirds of the employees eligible for early retirement left work before age sixty-five. Although the older employee—anybody over the age of forty—is protected by the Age Discrimination in Employment Act, many people approaching retirement age *are* forced out. It costs a lot of money to fight a company under the aegis of ADEA. It can be done, however. Chapter 9 discusses this important protective statute.

In effecting a true termination disguised as early retirement, the employer must remember that all other senior employees in the firm will know the details of the negotiations at once as soon as they have been confirmed. If the employer arranges a "deal" for a special worker, that same "deal" becomes a precedent for all other separations to come. The terms of the separation arrangement are thus extremely important on both sides of the fence. Guidelines appear in chapter 10.

If the employee refuses to take early retirement and rejects any kind of negotiated settlement offered, he or she may have to be terminated. However, the employee is still protected under the rules and regulations of ADEA. Any employer must be aware of the implications of that statute, particularly if the employee should decide to sue.

Bumping

"Bumping" is a chain reaction that takes place when an employer decides not to terminate anyone but rather to shift people about in order to make room for everyone—with one job less. There is no magic in it. In fact, it usually causes a great deal of grief in the personnel department just trying to keep track of workers who have changed jobs.

It is a practice disliked by unions and prohibited in many union contracts. The average employee may dislike bumping, too—for very good reasons.

Here's a typical example of bumping to avoid termination: Because of cutbacks in the work load, there are too many secretaries in the marketing department of a firm manufacturing clothes. One secretary has to go. In order not to fire anyone, the head of the department shifts the secretary with the least seniority to the stenography department. In the stenography department, the one with the least seniority is transferred to a job as tabulating clerk. In turn, one tabulating clerk is bumped to file clerk. This process continues until a job vacated by someone leaving the company voluntarily is available for filling.

Bumping might resemble several of the options open to the employer in the situation discussed earlier—creation of a new job for an employee who can't cut the mustard any longer and the addition of a new person to fill that employee's old job—but it isn't. In the case of bumping, the chain reaction usually continues until an empty spot shows up. The cost to the company remains the same in the long run. In creating a new slot for an underperforming executive, the company winds up with a larger payroll.

Attrition

In a larger company one frequently used alternative to termination is attrition. The word itself means to "wear down by rubbing against." However, when it is used in a business sense, it means a reduction in force through resignation, retirement, or death. In other words, the employer can allow an employee to remain with the company even when his or her job is no longer needed. Upon the appearance of a naturally occurring vacancy, the "assignmentless" employee can be shifted into that spot and retained there until it comes his or her own time to retire or leave voluntarily.

The disadvantage of attrition is that in times of economic downturn, when the company needs fewer and fewer employees, the rate of attrition does not speed up but remains the same as during times of economic prosperity. There tends to be a glut of underemployed workers and no way to get rid of them in order to streamline the company's operation to cope with the sagging economy.

Nevertheless, attrition is a valid method of coping with reductions in force when economic conditions warrant it.

Buyout

Certain employees do not have typical employee-employer relationships. That is, an employee may actually be a partner of the owner, providing services under terms of a contract. The employee may be an independent contractor, supplying a product that the company purchases without any physical control over the worker. The employee may be a franchiser who agrees to operate under certain rules and regulations. The employee may be a grantee, whose wages are supplied by government or foundation funds.

Most of these situations create problems when it comes to a decision to terminate. For example, the "partner" may become superfluous in the practical, everyday work situation. In that case, the "employer," or other partner, simply refers to the original contract creating the partnership and purchases his or her partner's half at cash value. This is called a "buyout."

The same type of situation exists with an employer who uses an independent contractor to supply goods or piecework materials. When it comes time for a cutback, the employer simply terminates the relationship. If there is no contract, the relationship can be terminated with a letter or a conversation. If there is a contract, the "employer" buys out the "employee" according to the terms of the contract.

The "employer" in a franchise situation does the same thing, working by the terms of the contract, buying out the franchiser or in some cases simply closing down the operation.

What the employer must note in this kind of situation is the all-important presence—or absence—of the contract. Such a contract must be adhered to point by point. A good contract will have been drawn up to cover such contingencies as economic downturns, slow sales, and so on.

No kind of termination is easy, but buying out a partner or buying out a supplier is more easily accomplished than terminating an employee, because everything is spelled out in writing and has been understood from the beginning of the relationship. It is simply a matter of working out the terms.

Note: The term *buyout* also refers to employer-employee relationships that exist without contracts. The buyout specifically means that the employee is offered a larger package in the event of termination than would normally be accorded under nondismissal conditions.

Termination—or Alternative Assignment?

The question naturally arises: If alternatives to termination are always available, why not simply move the employee into a new slot and continue as before? The question may sound simple, but it is a loaded one.

There are several causes for termination in which quick dismissal is preferable to any other option. They are:

- Absenteeism
- Lack of performance
- Blatant misconduct

There is no alternative answer to the question of absenteeism. When it becomes so manifest that it is causing the morale of the organization to sag, the guilty employee should be summarily dismissed.

Lack of performance or unsatisfactory performance is a second excellent reason for immediate dismissal. However, this moves into a gray area when a certain type of performance—let's say lifting heavy crates—may have become impossible for a person who has grown older or is less fit because of illness. Then, of course, the employee in question should be transferred to another position or allowed to opt for a new assignment.

Misconduct is a third situation in which there should be no alternative to termination. If an employee repeatedly disobeys orders in one situation, he or she is likely to disobey them in another. No possibility of alternative assignment should be considered.

For the rest of the cases—the natural aging of an employee, a change in fitness because of illness, a change in job specifications, a change in the employee's own mental health—the manager should try to figure out a place to assign the employee for the good of the company.

Issues of Performance, Discipline, and Economy

Whenever a termination is considered, the terminator should immediately review the terminatee's record at the company and ask himself or herself pertinent questions about the company's policies—to ascertain whether the employee *or the company* is most at fault. The questions should be divided into three categories: performance, discipline, and economy.

The following suggested questions to be answered whenever a termination is considered constitute a checklist to enable the employer to make the termination as fair, equitable, and honest as is humanly possible.

Questions on Issues of Performance

QUESTION: *Is the new employee carefully guided and monitored during the initial days of employment in order to evaluate attitude, ability, and skill at the job?*

ANSWER: The obvious time to identify any possible problems in performance is early on in the job. It is at this point that management should find out whether or not the new employee is capable of handling the job satisfactorily. A superior performance should also be noted at the same time, as a guide for future promotion or new assignments. The first days in the job are crucial from management's standpoint and should be used for an honest, critical analysis of the worker's present abilities and future potential within the company. The inferior as well as the superior employee must be assessed and earmarked at this point for future study.

QUESTION: *Has the specific job been defined in a proper way so that standards for performance can be clearly and accurately assessed?*

ANSWER: Nothing is more baffling to a newcomer to an organization than a job assignment without definite instructions and/or supervision by an able worker. Even the simplest job becomes a mystifying puzzle if it is not clearly explained. Every new employee must be questioned by someone in charge in order to find out if the points involved in the job have been communicated clearly enough to provide proper instruction. A worker with no idea of what a job is all about will never perform up to expectations.

QUESTION: *Has the employee been given adequate training and orientation to ensure success in the new job?*

ANSWER: Every organization has its own unique way of doing a given job. The employee, even though experienced in the working procedures of another company, will not know the special nuances and differences until conscientiously and carefully instructed. The most experienced worker will fail at a job if he or she is not given time to adapt to the special demands of the new requirements. Orientation and training go hand in hand. The worker must be allowed to settle into the job as well as into the company itself during the crucial first days. Otherwise, performance may never be satisfactory.

QUESTION: *In the event the employee is unable to perform the job properly, has he or she been instructed accordingly and allowed to correct errors or deficiencies in performance?*

ANSWER: The supervisor of the new employee must explain in detail every mistake or error detected in the new employee's performance, with specific pointers on how to achieve satisfactory performance. If the new employee is not told of errors or deficiencies, he or she assumes that the job is being done correctly. Small oversights and sloppy procedures must be spotted immediately; they may develop into larger mistakes and errors that will prevent the worker from ever attaining standard performance.

QUESTION: *If performance problems continue, have definite goals or objectives been set to help the worker attain acceptable performance?*
ANSWER: Inability to perform up to par may have many different causes. When the causes are corrected, the employee should be able to perform satisfactorily. The supervisor should set definite objectives for the employee to attain, without making the target too difficult to hit.

QUESTION: *Are evaluation appraisals carried out regularly in a fair and accurate manner so as to indicate the employee's true abilities and attitudes?*
ANSWER: Although many employees resist evaluation and performance analysis, claiming it resembles grades given to schoolchildren, such "grades" must be given from time to time in order to measure the effectiveness of the employee's performance. Even in a small company, such evaluation records must be kept to create an accurate profile of each employee.

QUESTION: *Are evaluations carefully made, or are they simply whitewashes of mediocre performance abilities?*
ANSWER: An evaluation means nothing if it is not accurate and honest. A glowing appraisal of a mediocre worker may stroke the worker's ego, but it does not alert him or her to the fact that performance should be improved. Likewise, too harsh an appraisal can just as easily puncture the worker's ego and destroy confidence. A worker who is headed for a fall should be alerted to the fact in advance.

QUESTION: *Are the same standards used to evaluate all workers in the same job description?*
ANSWER: If two workers who are performing essentially the same job about equally well find that they are not being appraised equally, one will feel cheated, the other overconfident. Although it is difficult for the evaluator to judge everyone equally,

he or she should try to make the judgments as equitable and fair as possible.

QUESTION: *Are certain errors in performance overlooked in some workers and not in others?*
ANSWER: Favoritism is a human failing that is present in every level of the work force. Errors that are noted in one worker should not be overlooked in another doing the same job. Inequity of this nature not only destroys objectivity and creates animosity among individual workers but also tends to undermine the morale of all workers.

Questions on Issues of Discipline

QUESTION: *Are the rules and regulations involving discipline clearly defined and communicated to all employees, either by personnel manuals or bulletin board postings?*
ANSWER: Rules and regulations must be clear, enforceable, relevant to the job situation, and reasonable. They must either be posted where they can always be seen or issued to each employee and identified as "must reading." Any special rules—dress codes, smoking rules, drinking regulations, and so on—must be clearly spelled out and easy to understand. The rules must be enforceable as well, not nuisance items that cannot be monitored. An unreasonable rule is usually ignored and sets a bad precedent in company discipline across the board. Rules and regulations are not attempts to bring workers into line; they are provided to make working together reasonably comfortable and safe for all employees.

QUESTION: *Does the punishment fit the crime?*
ANSWER: A minor infraction should receive a minor reprimand, a major infraction a major reprimand. Discipline should fit the offense not only in its scope but in its general tone as well. Rules and regulations too strict and unreasonable, with punishment enormously out of line, must be corrected.

QUESTION: *Is the disciplinary program progressive in intent, with harsher penalties for repeated rule violations?*
ANSWER: A program of progressive discipline (discussed in detail in chapter 5) is a must in any organization. Not only does

it provide documentation for legal cases, but it has a positive effect on company morale.

QUESTION: *Is discipline enforced uniformly, or is it meted out at the whim of the supervisor?*
ANSWER: Wherever human beings involve themselves in collective action, as they do in the work force, there are personality differences and human likes and dislikes. The supervisor must try to be objective in the enforcement of disciplinary actions, at least as objective as is possible. Discrimination must be avoided at all costs, or it will come back to haunt the supervisor. Management must watch out for outbreaks of racial tension, violation of women's rights, ethnic slurs, and other such behavior—all of which can be held against a company in the exacting of disciplinary actions. Supervisors must be selected for their ability to rise above personality clashes, favoritism, and specific dislikes.

QUESTION: *Have other workers been disciplined or terminated for a particular offense in the past, or is the disciplinary act in question the first of its kind?*
ANSWER: Management can be in big trouble when it suddenly does an about-face and decides to prosecute an infraction that has been overlooked in the past. There are plenty of reasons for "making an issue out of *this* offense," but if the offense has never been punished in the past, it must be reasonably publicized and discussed *before* the first disciplinary action is taken. Precedent occurs in the work force as well as in judicial rulings. If the precedent in the past was to overlook offense A, it will be extremely difficult to enforce the rule regarding offense A in the future unless the offense A rule is advertised as enforceable in the future and the violation is then consistently condemned as "a bad thing." The same is true in reverse: the sudden nonenforcement of a rule regarding Offense B can be puzzling and arbitrary, too.

QUESTION: *What are you really disciplining an employee for— what you* say *you are, or what you* do not *say you are?*
ANSWER: Motive is a tricky business. An employer may say that an employee is being fired for unsatisfactory performance. It may even be true that the employee is performing unsatisfactorily. However, the *real* reason the employer is firing the em-

ployee may have nothing to do with performance; rather, it might have to do with the fact that a supervisor tried to date a subordinate and she turned him down. If performance is truly unsatisfactory, an employer can usually make a termination stand up. However, if a claim of unsatisfactory performance can be demonstrated to be patently untrue, then the employer may be proved a liar and found to have fired the employee because she spurned his advances. Management must be able to prove its motive in any case of termination.

QUESTION: *Is termination of an employee actually the last resort?*

ANSWER: It is possible that if a worker fails to perform satisfactorily, he or she may work better in a different job assignment, in another department, or in a simpler and lower-echelon job. Alternatives to termination were discussed earlier in this chapter.

Questions on Issues of Economy

QUESTION: *Can hiring be curtailed or stopped completely to let attrition help reduce bloated payrolls in an economic downturn?*

Answer: Reduction in force is the usual reaction to a change in the economy that affects a company's sales revenues and future orders. Terminated workers rarely come back. Management must realize that for every discharged employee, a great deal of time, money, and effort are completely wasted. In the case of a company still hiring some people while at the same time firing others to reduce the work force, it is obvious that a halt should be made to acquiring new people until the economy stabilizes. There is much to be said for letting attrition—the natural reduction in force through voluntary means such as retirement and job changing—take its course.

QUESTION: *Can the organization function on reduced hours or a four-day week with corresponding payroll deductions?*

ANSWER: The Equal Employment Opportunities Commission recently suggested this method of cutting back to avoid mass firings and considered the matter fair and equitable because all workers are affected equally. In such a move, management must cut down on higher-echelon executive salaries as well as worker wages. This avoid the possibility that a terminated employee will find some reason for bringing suit against the company for discriminatory firing or for termination against the "public policy."

QUESTION: *Can payroll overhead costs be cut in order to keep from having to fire large numbers of employees?*

ANSWER: Management should look at a number of cost-cutting options before deciding on a specific reduction in force. For example, insurance benefit levels can easily be reduced, as long as the employees know about it and are given the option of continuing them at the present rate and reducing the number of employees. Insurance costs can also be transferred to employees in order to save both money and jobs. Employees should be allowed to decide on such moves.

QUESTION: *How is the reduction in force going to be administered? Is it logical or hit-and-miss?*

ANSWER: In most cases of reduction in force, the procedure is to terminate employees with the least working seniority. That is, the last in are the first out. There is also a secondary method—that of targeting certain departments and simply eliminating them or of targeting certain jobs and eliminating them. A combination of these two methods—reduction by seniority *and* targeting of jobs—can prove effective, too. In whatever way it is effected, management must let the work force know exactly how the termination procedure is administered. In the execution, care must be taken to adhere strictly to seniority and/or job targeting so that no employee can claim discrimination or raise "public policy" issues.

QUESTION: *Is the company trying to force early retirements?*

ANSWER: Although early retirement is a legitimate alternative to termination, it must be a voluntary inducement to the employees and not an involuntary decision forced upon them. The same is true of certain issues of unsatisfactory performance that are actually trumped-up and used as false reasons for riffing. Such procedures can backfire badly on management and cause morale problems. They can also blow up into discrimination charges and result in the filing of many court suits.

CHAPTER 7

Outplacement Assistance

When Mark Andrews introduced Jim Young to Ronald Simpson in case history number 4, Young entered a brand new world—the world of outplacement assistance. He had never before been forced to look for a job while unemployed. In fact, he had been hired at Maddon, Inc., while still working at a previous job. He had never before been on the streets looking for a job—except for his initial employment effort. He had spent his life working, not seeking employment.

Andrews knew how hard it would be for Young to land a new job. For an individual in such a high echelon of management, the possibilities of getting an equal or better job were quite small—particularly since the niche Young occupied was so very high. Outplacement assistance therefore seemed the best bet to Andrews.

He was right. Young would have been hard put to figure out on his own how to proceed in looking for work. However, in the hands of Ronald Simpson, he proceeded to rethink his career, look over the field, and decide on a slightly different approach to employment. He had setbacks in this process, as almost everyone involved in outplacement does, but in the end—six months later—he finally went to work for another manufacturing firm, this time in charge of a production section a great deal smaller than the one at Maddon. His particular talent for dealing directly with machine operators came in handy in his new job, which involved heading up an experimental research-and-development type of division.

Although the steps through which Young went in his outplacement adventure had nothing to do with his termination at Maddon—except that outplacement was used in order to help him after termination and at Maddon's expense—they are important for any terminator to understand before proposing an outgoing executive for such assistance.

What Outplacement Can Do for the Employer

In the words of one outplacer:

> Outplacement enables employers to provide career relocation assistance to dismissed employees as part of their severance arrangements. As such, outplacement serves as a management tool, both to facilitate the necessary organizational change and to treat the employee with some compassion.

In order to be considered successful, a good outplacement firm should:

- Smooth the termination process.
- Reduce the chance of lawsuits.
- Improve employer-employee relations.
- Enhance company morale.
- Improve the image of the company.
- Aid in restructuring a company to improve productivity and profitability.
- Solve problems of promotion.
- Channel communication between employee and employer.
- Reduce the cost of termination.

Smoothing the Termination Process

A good outplacer helps smooth the process of termination by working with members of management even before the employee has been told he or she is out. The outplacement specialist can help the management representative determine the best way to handle the discharge. With proper counseling, the employer can determine:

1. When to fire the employee.
2. Who should be responsible for the firing.
3. Other specifics that are frequently dodged by management.

Addressing the Problem of Lawsuits

An outplacer can help any company reduce the chance of appeals and lawsuits by assuring the discharged employee that he or she will receive professional help in finding a new position. The outplacer can also advise management on specific issues that might become possible danger spots in case of discrimination or public policy concerns. And by acting as a lightning rod for the terminated employee's animosity, the outplacer can help "ground" any possible reprisals.

Improving Employer-Employee Relations

The simple fact of the outplacer's presence during a termination becomes a good public relations ploy. It proves to the other employees that management is concerned about all its workers. Good public relations is important for any large company, especially if it is involved heavily in community and customer service.

Enhancing Company Morale

Company morale is always an important factor, particularly when there is a reduction in force or a reorganization that involves the dismissal of a large number of people. Outplacement can help keep morale high, even though the number of officers and workers dismissed during such an upheaval may be in the hundreds. The presence of the outplacer proves to the employees remaining that management does have a heart after all.

Polishing Up the Company Image

The smooth functioning of a model outplacement team looks good not only to the employees of the company but also to those on the outside looking on. During a reorganization or a reduction in force, workers who are not attached to the company keep a wary eye out to see how the demotions and firings are handled. So does the public. Huge headlines charging inept riffing and slaughterhouse tactics do not improve sales of the company's products among working people. A good outplacer's presence puts the firm in an excellent light.

Restructuring to Improve Productivity and Profitability

The termination of an employee may well be part of a company's attempt to increase its productivity. By weeding out executives who are only marginal performers and retaining good performers, the company increases profitability as well. An obvious consequence is a growing need to deal with the separation of executives and managers as well as entire departments and divisions. The presence of an outplacer can immeasurably help the restructuring of a company to improve profits.

Solving Problems of Promotion

Productivity and profitability are not the only things helped by a good outplacer; inherent problems of promotion among the remaining personnel can be solved, too, by judicious pruning through riffing and the subsequent promotion of various remaining officers into the vacated spots. Wise promotion moves enhance the company's outside image and inside morale.

Channeling Employer-Employee Communication

The outplacer can act as a channel of communication between the discharged employee and his or her former employer until the individual is relocated. This is an important link in employer-employee relations, which can get particularly sticky during a termination, when emotional reactions are at a critical level. By neutralizing the antipathy, guilt, rage, and pain, the outplacer can make the relationship almost bearable.

Reducing the Cost of Termination

An outplacer can actually reduce the cost of the termination procedure by advising management on the structuring of severance benefits, including how much pay to award a dismissed employee, whether benefits should be continued after termination and for how long, and whether the employee should be allowed to use office facilities.

In the long run, not only does the use of outplacement assistance help management reduce potential economic and legal problems involved with termination, but it also provides a chance to treat the dismissed employee more humanely.

What Outplacement Can Do for the Employee

The purpose of the outplacement program is, as one outplacer explains, "to soften the blow of being fired. Outplacement acts as a buffer between what has happened—the termination—and what will happen to the employee."

During a recession, almost 90 percent of all employees are dismissed because of mergers and acquisitions or personality conflicts—*not* because of poor performance. As a consequence, a white-collar executive is not only surprised by the termination but is also unprepared to cope with the rigors of job hunting. The thought of a long, tough search is beyond his or her comprehension. The first and most crucial point in a typical outplacement scenario is: *Get the former employee into outplacement immediately.*

Once that element of the outplacement procedure is taken care of, there are a number of important points that the average outplacement program is prepared to handle:

- Support during the stages of termination.
- Assistance in developing a family budget to cope with the job search.
- Minimization of trauma to the family through goal-setting conferences.
- An assessment of career strengths and weaknesses.
- An identification of marketable skills.
- Isolation of suitable job markets for targeting.
- Development of a marketing strategy identifying appropriate job markets.
- A program for penetrating various job markets.
- Preparation of résumés and letters to prospective employers.
- Mass mailing to designated employers.
- Training in securing job interviews.
- Development of interview skills.
- Coaching in one-on-one dialogue techniques.
- Techniques for conducting salary negotiations.
- Methods of developing and establishing personal contacts with executives.
- Support throughout the entire job search.

Outplacement's help for the employee is not limited simply to hand holding and guidance through the jungle of employment opportunities but can also involve help in other special ways when needed. For example, a sloppy dresser may be taught how to upgrade grooming. There are numerous other details that might come up to be taken care of. Yet guidance is the outplacer's main reason for being.

In general, the outplacer tries to assess the job strengths and weaknesses of the terminated individual in order to build up a program that will enhance and feature the employee's good qualities and abilities. In some cases, the outplacer may even find new work areas for the employee to explore.

How Outplacement Works

Through the fifteen years of the existence of outplacement assistance, the concept has been honed and fine-tuned into an effective tool for management to make termination less traumatic and destructive to its employees. In those fifteen years it has settled down into a fairly routine process.

Outplacement starts immediately after termination has been effected. During the termination interview, the outplacer sits in an adjoining room waiting for the ax to fall. Once the exit interview is concluded, the employer who has performed the termination tells the employee that he or she will be working with the outplacer from that moment on.

The terminator then takes the former employee into the adjoining room, introduces the outplacer, and leaves. The terminatee is now in the hands of the outplacer and his or her team of associates. That means that the terminatee does not physically return to the office at all, except to clean the desk out soon after the exit interview. From then on, employment is a thing of the past; it is *reemployment* and a new future that are of concern.

To emphasize the complete break with the past, the outplacer takes the terminated employee in hand and introduces him or her to an entirely new physical environment—a kind of way station between jobs. The former employee will be using the new facilities to make and receive telephone calls; to write and receive letters;.to write, transcribe, and print résumés; to work on interviews; and to do all the other things necessary to prepare himself or herself for the job hunt.

The outplacer's way station usually provides separate cubbyholes for individual job seekers to use—complete with telephones, writing materials, a typewriter, and note pads to take down addresses during telephone conversations. Each former employee will also have access to secretarial assistance for the duration of his or her stay at the way station.

The change in scene is a needed break in the psychological rhythm of the former employee's life. The outplacer must take care to impress on the former employee that all his or her energies must now be directed toward getting a new job, not toward brooding over the past or keeping in contact with old associates. The emphasis is on the future.

The Four Phases of Outplacement

The process of outplacement has four main phases:
- Neutralizing the trauma.
- Rebuilding the ego.
- Planning the job campaign.
- Knocking on doors.

Neutralizing the Trauma

The first phase takes about two or three days. When any individual is fired, he or she feels inadequate, insecure, rejected, and in need of sympathy and emotional support. What the terminated employee requires immediately is a helping hand, someone who can lead him or her through the harrowing and frightening emotional stages.

In turn, neutralization is divided up into three separate mini-phases:

- Ventilation
- Mourning
- Burial

Ventilation

By the time the terminated employee has been informed of the discharge and has been introduced to the outplacer, he or she has usually recovered from the immediate shock and disbelief. Once the terminatee understands that he or she is indeed being discharged, there is a brief period of rage.

Outplacers learn to handle this emotional outburst—called "ventilation" in the jargon of the trade—as sympathetically as possible. Outrage and anger are usually short-lived; no one can sustain them for long. Once these emotions have run their course, they are followed by depression and hopelessness, as will be discussed below.

Mourning

After ventilation comes a realization and acceptance of the finality of the situation. The employee is out of work. There is no other way to look at it.

"It's a period of mourning, a wake for the old job," one outplacer says. "As [the former employee] talks it out, we start guiding the conversation around to the fact that while he deserves to feel hurt and angry—this isn't a sign of weakness but humanness—he doesn't deserve to feel hurt and angry forever."

This is the beginning of counseling. Along with this beginning, the outplacer then reminds the terminatee that he or she has practical problems that must be faced: among them, breaking the news to his or her family, friends, and associates. It is during this part of the outplacement process that the specialist must tread carefully. It is the onset of depression and hopelessness that can cause the most trouble. Coupled with depression is a feeling of fear and anguish.

A former employee may want the outplacer to follow him or her home while the terminatee tells the spouse what has happened. An outplacer may indeed opt to accompany the terminated worker when he or she breaks the bad news to the spouse. "Most spouses are very supportive," one outplacer says. "But others are disasters. They start yelling and moaning about how they're going to lose the house. A person under that kind of pressure is going to accept the first job offer, even if it isn't the right job or the best terms negotiable."

It is a temptation at this point for the former employee to take the severance pay and get lost on some desert island or in Las Vegas or Atlantic City for a few weeks. "That's always a mistake," according to one outplacer. "Four weeks on a beach, with nothing to do but brood, only leaves a person more bitter than ever."

Burial

Within seventy-two hours the former employee is usually ready to bury the past and accept the fact that there is a brand new future out there in store for him or her—one that may not exactly be wonderful at the moment but that may be someday.

Anger and depression are interred and hopefully forgotten. By now the period of neutralization should be over and done with.

Rebuilding the Ego

Phase two begins as soon as the terminatee has gone through the emotional upheaval of anger and mourning. This phase is much longer than the initial phase. One outplacer calls it the "positive orientation program." It begins with a typical diversionary tactic of a psychological nature.

This diversion is an enormous questionnaire, which is actually a guideline for a long summary of the individual's career. It requires thoughtful, yet concise, answers and takes about two or three days to fill out. The outplacer explains:

> It gives a person a sense that things are starting to happen. Also, the questionnaire gives us a lot of information about the individual's specific professional accomplishments that we can use to write up an impressive résumé. And some of the questions we ask, such as, "What kind of work do you most want to do now?" force the employee to put the past behind him and start thinking about the future.

Filling out the questionnaire and creating a retrospective of his or her business life can also help the former employee put the recent developments into a proper perspective. The average employee can see that he or she has indeed been able to accomplish things in the past, despite the recent firing. Looking back in this context can help the former employee see into the future by realizing that he or she does have potential.

During this important phase of outplacement, the outplacer tries to persuade the terminated employee that the termination was not completely his or her own fault. "Getting fired," one outplacer explains, "is seldom the result of simple incompetence. It is much more commonly the result of personality conflicts; poor corporate management, which often puts capable individuals in the wrong jobs; and such corporate maneuvers as mergers, cutbacks, or the closing of facilities."

Another outplacer says: "There is a growing awareness of the no-fault character of termination. It's like a no-fault divorce. Can you really say who was to blame? There is less emphasis on placing blame than on getting both parties separated with as little damage to both sides as possible."

Planning the Job Campaign

With ventilation completed and with the former employee's ego back together, the outplacer now moves the out-of-work individual into the third phase of outplacement. This consists of outlining a plan of attack—a "campaign"—with the job seeker as the "candidate" and the job as the "target."

Because the candidate has been working for so long, job hunting is an unfamiliar project. Most people with long working careers know very little about looking for work. The project is equated with a marketing campaign. The worker is, in effect, a product to be marketed. And as a product, he or she must be "packaged correctly," "targeted" for the right slot, with proper market "penetration" in mind.

Packaging is the important exercise of the campaign. The executive who has been working for years may not have paid much attention to personal appearance. Usually he or she will dress instinctively to emulate co-workers. An outplacer may find that the candidate's dress is not right to project the effective job-seeking image. The object of dressing for job finding is to "blend in," not stand out. Also, a candidate with gray hair may be urged to get the gray out by coloring the hair darker. "Youthful-looking people get hired first," one outplacer has observed.

The Hard-Sell Résumé

In addition to appearance, the "product" is counseled in preparing a hard-sell résumé that will feature the most salable of his or her skills and achievements. Producing a satisfactory résumé is not quite so easy as most executives think. Usually a résumé expert on the outplacement team will look over the draft and offer suggestions. The idea of the résumé is to encapsule the most important of an employee's achievements and abilities and present them in readable, inspiring style. The paper must be a definite hard-sell, with the candidate's best features headlined and exploited to the hilt.

The Mock Interview

Once the résumé is in shape, the candidate is ready for a trial run. What follows is a mock interview with a prospective employer. But this is a dry run with a difference: the mock interview is staged with a video camera picking up the entire dialogue.

Once the interview is completed, a team of outplacement counselors view the videotape of it and make notes on the good and bad points—in private, without the candidate's presence. These informal critiques concern personal appearance, negative mannerisms, attitudes that come across detrimentally, vocal no-nos—all discussed openly and without inhibition. For instance:

> He's trying to play the cool cat, but all he seems to be doing is playing coy. There's no way he's going to fool some of these personnel managers. He's outdated. Also, he keeps picking his nose. That's really a sign of carelessness. He pops his eyes when he talks about his accomplishments. It makes them come across as fabrications.

After the outplacement team's critical rundown on the candidate, he or she is called in and presented with the findings, albeit in a slightly watered down version. The idea of this critique is not to undermine the candidate's self-assurance but to give him or her pointers on correcting lapses or negative qualities in the performance.

For example, he or she may appear too aggressive, too superficial, or too much the laid-back know-it-all. Or the candidate may click his or her teeth, purse lips, tug earlobes, or fumble with buttons.

A typical outplacer's report to a candidate sounds like this:

> Watch yourself here. You'll see that you're trying to impress by appearing the strong, silent authoritarian figure. The person hiring you doesn't know what's on your mind. You have to tell him or her what you're thinking about. Now you saw yourself with that finger to the nose. Please don't. And I don't think that mannerism helps much, either. Can you talk without letting your eyes open and sparkle? It's embarrassing to discuss tics like this—but they don't make you look good. Also, they undermine your integrity. They make you look like an actor playing a role.

What to Do, What Not

Then a list of dos and don'ts is made up for the candidate. The candidate studies them and runs through another interview, making every attempt possible to correct errors and damaging mannerisms. Depending on the candidate, one rerun may be enough. Several run-throughs may be necessary to overcome particularly difficult problems. By the time the candidate is through the final replay, he or she should be close to letter-perfect in attitude and manner.

Knocking on Doors

After two or three weeks of intensive preparation, the candidate is deemed ready to hit the bricks and try to swing open a few doors.

One outplacer assesses the job market the candidate will face like this:

> There are two job markets. The first is the open market, which means jobs that are open and waiting to be filled. Companies often go to executive-search firms to fill these slots, but the headhunters are reluctant to propose an unemployed man. They should sometimes, but they won't. That's why we aim at the second market, which we call the hidden market, consisting of jobs that do not yet exist.

The fourth phase of outplacement operates on those two job market levels.

The Open Market

For the open market, the candidate is asked to search his or her own memory, files, Christmas card list, alumni association roster, and so on for the names of any contacts who might be useful in the job search.

Copies of the candidate's résumé are sent out to all the names on this master list. In addition, résumés are sent out to conventional scattershot recipients—employment agencies, executive recruiters, help-wanted box numbers, addresses of firms in the yellow pages in the proper corporate area, and so on.

From the open market a few nibbles may come. The candidate should pursue them immediately, using every trick and stratagem he or she can think of to impress a potential employer.

The Hidden Market

Nevertheless, it is the secret market that holds the most promise. This is the market of unadvertised jobs. The reason the jobs are unadvertised is that they are not yet open. This market is the rather extensive warehouse of "future" positions; the holders of these jobs are underachievers who do not know their jobs may soon be up for grabs.

Management is actively searching behind the scenes for replacements for the holders of these particular jobs, without letting the job holders know it. Key personnel in the company are on the lookout for possible candidates.

This is the job market that the outplacer trains the candidate to exploit to the fullest degree. The outplacer counsels him or her on how to approach such executives. It is a tricky business, because there is no job listing, and the person doing the actual search is never named because the search is clandestine.

Scanning the hidden market is usually tackled in three steps:

• Preparation of a list of companies with opportunities the candidate is seeking.
• Specific search for employees in the target companies as a means of developing contacts.
• Interview with potential employer through the side or back door.

It goes like this: The candidate prepares a list of a number of corporations or smaller companies that have job categories conforming to his or her particular qualifications. Although this list must be of a practical length, it should also be wide-ranging. Since this is a blindman's bluff, the more possibilities there are, the better.

Once the list is complete, the candidate goes back to old files or searches his or her memory for names of people who work at, say, target A. Perhaps all the candidate's acquaintances have moved on. If unable to establish direct contact with anyone at target A, he or she then gets through to someone who *knows* an employee at target A, proceeding from Jones to Smith to Johnson at target A.

After being introduced to a contact at target A by a friend or acquaintance, the candidate takes the target A contact to lunch for a friendly chat. The candidate does not mention the fact that he or she is unemployed but merely tries to find out something about company policy and personnel. What the candidate is primarily interested in is the identity of the key person at target A, the one with the clout, the real mover and shaker at the company. That is the person who will actually be doing the hiring for the job the candidate has his or her eye on.

Using this contact, the candidate tries to set up a meeting with the mover and shaker. By manufacturing all kinds of excuses to see him or her, the candidate finally arranges a meeting, particularly after making friends with the contact and using his or her casual friendship to make the final approach.

The interview with the mover and shaker includes no specific mention of wanting a job. The approach used may be something like this:

"I'm looking for a new assignment in your industry. I have certain skills I know would be useful. I realize you don't have any job available. However, I would be appreciative if you could give me ten minutes to tell me how you see the needs of the industry."

During the interview, the candidate keeps mentioning all the things he or she has done with the hope that it will touch off something in the target's mind—that he or she might either be able to use the candidate or know someone else in the industry who could.

Tapping the hidden market is a difficult procedure, but it is the best move for a high-echelon executive in need of a specific kind of job.

Weathering Bouts of Discouragement

Once the candidate starts opening doors and interviewing, he or she checks in on a regular basis with the outplacer in charge to discuss progress or lack of it. There is usually a sixth-week slump when the candidate becomes discouraged from lack of results. By this time the candidate has no hope for the future.

"We train him and develop his strategy and put him in the ring," one outplacer says. "We stay in his corner and give him advice between rounds. We put a patch on his eye; we tell him what he's doing wrong. But he's got to do his own fighting."

And the candidate usually learns to cope with his new challenges. By the time the six-week slump has passed, the grass looks greener, the skies look bluer, and it's obvious that there is a job out there somewhere to be had for the taking.

The Cost of Outplacement

Although there are no specific rules on the amount an outplacer charges for his or her services, it may be somewhere in the neighborhood of 15 percent of the employee's base salary, assuming the salary is more than thirty thousand dollars. Below that salary level, the minimum fee for outplacement services is approximately forty-five hundred dollars.

Usually, the employer is not billed until after the candidate first meets with the outplacer and the outplacer determines whether or not the two of them can work together.

Normally an employee earning a salary of twenty thousand dollars or less is able to find another job without too much trouble. A terminated employee in that job range isn't in need of the specific expertise of an outplacer. "We're not being snobs about this, but it typically just isn't cost-effective to call in outplacement help" in the case of the employee in the lower salary ranges.

The Role of Outplacement

Outplacement, in short, is a specialized science that has become a familiar part of the modern corporate structure, in small as well as large companies. The technique of helping terminated employees get new jobs requires a specialized working knowledge of corporate life and life-style.

It requires a comprehension of job functions, of the workings of various levels of the work force, of the way to approach the hidden job market, of current business conditions, of human psychology, and of the effective application of communications and interpersonal skills.

If handled properly, outplacement can be a rewarding experience for the individual who must get another job as well as for the company forced to part with the terminatee for any reason whatsoever.

CHAPTER 8

Appealing the Termination

EVEN THOUGH the termination of an employee for unsatisfactory performance or simple reduction in force is considered the final step, many corporations operate informal systems of appeal involving individual "judges" within the company. Others use built-in appeal systems of a more formal nature that allow a terminated person to plead for reinstatement.

A number of the more informal appeal systems allow any employee with a gripe to seek out a person at the top of the chain of command—even the president of the company in some instances—to have his or her termination reviewed.

Another system allows the terminated employee to call in a third party to make a final decision after hearing both sides of the story. This system may operate through the company's personnel department, using a member of the department who might be considered as "objective as possible," even though the "judge" is a member of the establishment.

A more formal concept involves a company's grievance program run in conjunction with its progressive discipline system. The disciplinary apparatus can be used to review the case of a terminated employee who wants to appeal a dismissal, even after the resources of the grievance system have been totally exhausted.

Typically, this type of built-in appeal system is modeled on the kind of program instituted by the country's unions in the years just following World War II. Such a system involves an adversary relationship between management and union, with the employee being represented by the union counsel and management by a company counsel. The appeal thus becomes a kind of court appearance between employee and firm, with the decision made by judges who include union and management representatives.

If no system exists, either formal or informal, a company may allow an employee to consult a professional arbitrator in order to have his or her problem aired in a formal fashion. Professional arbitration is an excellent tool for the small company to use when it wants to be as fair as possible to its employees.

The last resort for an appeal of termination is the formal court system.

The Two Basic Types of Appeal Systems

Generally speaking, there are two types of appeal systems in current use by nonunion companies both large and small. They can be divided roughly into *informal* systems and *formal* systems.

To differentiate formal and informal, let's assume that "formal" refers to a type of appeal system based on or resembling the union appeal system mentioned earlier, one set up for review of union-management cases. In it, both union and management are bound by contract; the "formality" exists because a contract implies legality and law. Thus the formal system here involves concrete steps within the clauses of a contract or within the parameters of a set of rules and regulations on company policy—steps resembling the union system. Let's also assume that "informal" refers to a system that is not connected with a written contract and that is not based on a typical union appeal system. Thus "formal" could mean both a system with a contract and a system *resembling* one involving a contract.

Typical Informal Appeal Systems

Typically, the informal appeal system is a hit-and-miss affair involving a presumably objective person in the firm in a position off the firing line who can, it is hoped, see both sides of a possible dispute between two people at different echelons within the company.

The Open-Door Policy

The idea of the open-door policy came about first just after World War II as a reaction against the military system of forcing all matters to go "through channels"—that is, up a chain of command through each superior, step by step to another and another, and so on to the top. The obvious disadvantage of the "through channels" approach is the fact that no lower-echelon worker's complaint will ever reach a high enough level to effect action.

The open-door policy is an attempt by management to let an employee from any level of the company make a final appeal to an executive near or at the top of the company hierarchy. Critics of the system point out that because this is set up initially as an artificial situation, the terminated person's chances of winning a reinstatement are minuscule indeed. The top management official, supposedly objective, is, of course, far from that, inasmuch as he or she represents the establishment, and it is a member of the establishment who has decided to terminate the employee, who, when terminated, is no longer a member of the establishment.

As such, critics note, the open-door policy is only an attempt to give the lower-level employee the *feeling* that there is a kind of justice in the operation of the firm.

Proponents of the system regard the open-door policy as an excellent one for clearing the air after friction between employees. They also like to argue that a higher-echelon individual will have much less bias toward management than a lower-echelon one. The policy has long been touted in management books and is an established method of affording appeals to employees with grievances.

Theoretically, at least, the open-door policy should be an excellent way for the unjustly terminated employee to seek redress. However, for some reason, it has not been quite so successful in practice as was originally hoped. Most employees do not, in fact, ever make use of the open-door policy to air their grievances. One executive says that he thinks it is because the typical worker considers it a "management gimmick" to make the higher-ups look good.

Actually, the open-door policy is in no way a formal court of last resort, nor does it constitute any system by which grievances can be aired for appeal. It is simply and quite honestly a system set up to provide a place for an employee to gripe, to discuss personal problems, and to complain about management or work rules. In no way does it imply any promise to reform management, the company, or anyone in it.

"Some employees," writes Robert Coulson, author of *The Termination Handbook*, Free Press, 1981, "may suspect that the open door leads to the back door, that a complainer will be marked as a troublemaker, that supervisors resent any use of the procedure."

But at least the open-door system allows the terminated employee a chance to discuss his or her discharge with someone on a higher level. Certain terminated employees have indeed been reinstated after such a discussion. However, the system is not a formal grievance process of the type instituted to hear union complaints.

The Ombudsman System

One former employee described events leading up to his termination like this:

> I always got along with my old boss very well. But when he was transferred to another division of the company, I was assigned to a newcomer on the scene. He was very hard to get along with. He didn't know much at all and was trying to bluff his way through. And he kept taking it out on the people who worked under him. He kept picking on me until I had to fight back. I shouldn't have lost my temper and told him off, but I did. He fired me for it. Who could I go to for any kind of appeal? He was as much at fault as I was, maybe more. I felt the company was wrong in not having someone up there to go to for proper judgment.

Because many employees feel exactly the same as the one quoted above, some corporations began to create posts for authoritarian figures who could be approached for judgmental decisions. This uninvolved third party was called an "ombudsman." Although the term began to lose out after some years, the ombudsman system is still an excellent one.

The ombudsman is primarily an individual—like a parent figure—who is required to remain totally uninvolved, both personally and managerially, with the company and who can act as an objective arbiter when an individual wants to appeal a decision considered unfair or out of line. The ombudsman may be required to settle an argument between two top-level executives, or he or she may be required to make a decision on a misunderstanding between two very low-level workers.

The ombudsman is the ideal third party to decide on a termination action in an appeal between worker and supervisor. The ombudsman system works well with a smaller or medium-sized company that does not have the resources to set up a formal system of appeal.

Typical Formal Appeal Systems

Many corporations have devised appeal systems to take care of nonunion employees who feel that they are being treated unfairly, although not all have. Some disguise the appeal system under the heading "human resources committee." The idea of treating the employee as a resource is appealing to the image makers in business today. The employee becomes a "valuable property," to use another buzz phrase.

The human resources touch can be admirable when applied to a truly objective appeal situation. The employee is able to confront the superior to determine exactly why he or she has been terminated. The superior is required to explain in detail, and document point by point, the reasons the employee has been discharged. If the superior's case is weak, the employee may well be reinstated. If so, he or she will usually be put back to work for *another* supervisor.

Ordinarily, in a company that has a built-in formal appeal system, it is the lower-echelon nonunion employee and perhaps an occasional middle-echelon white-collar worker who are mostly concerned with its use. For middle management and top management, the system is simply not set up in such a way that its use can be effective.

Another disadvantage of the formal appeal system is that other than in large companies, such a system is usually too cumbersome to handle. In other words, the situation doesn't come up often enough to warrant all the trouble of setting up the complicated mechanism for handling it. For the smaller company, an alternative to the formal appeal system is usually the use of some other method.

Model for the Formal Appeal System

Typically the company that sets up its own appeal system, particularly in reference to appeals of termination, usually models it in detail according to the progressive discipline and grievance system already discussed in chapter 5.

To recapitulate it briefly: The progressive discipline and grievance system involves a program in which an employee of counseling, reprimand, appeal, warning, and so on, throughout his or her working days.

The five main steps in the typical progressive discipline system are:

1. Counseling
2. Written reprimands
3. Appeals
4. Final warning
5. Termination

As has been noted, steps 2 and 3, "written reprimand" and "appeal," may be repeated several times before step 4, "final warning." Once step 5, "termination," occurs, the appeal system can review steps 2 and 3, judging the case from the evidence in the written warnings and other evaluational material.

A firm with a well-functioning grievance system can utilize that machinery for hearing cases of terminated employees who want to get another chance. Both terminator and terminatee must prepare documented cases for themselves and bring in witnesses or supporters for the hearings that take place.

The appeal stage built into the basic progressive discipline system can also be used to serve as a model for a more extended system to hear both sides of a case of termination by the simiple addition of a sixth step to the basic five: terminal appeal.

There is naturally a drawback to the use of the grievance system for appeal. By the time the individuals involved in the original termination have worked themselves up to a decision to fire, it is rare indeed that they will reverse themselves and decide to retain the employee.

However, it has happened. Nevertheless, because the grievance system does work well, such a step can lead to a further and more objective appeal—the use of an outside arbitrator to judge the case employing the machinery of the grievance program.

The Arbitration System

Although it is not an approach in widespread use, some corporations have set up appeal systems that wind up in in-house arbitration sessions. Typically, such a system hears last-resort complaints against termination as well as other less serious disciplinary actions. Although the system is called an "arbitration" process, the "arbitrator" is usually not one individual but a group of officers, possibly including a member of management, a disinterested representative of lower-level employment, and a co-worker selected by the terminated employee to help his or her case.

Arbitration proceeds along the line of a typical small claims court: the plaintiff (the terminated employee) presents his or her case; the defendant (the terminator) presents his or her case; and the board decides for or against the plaintiff.

Such an appeal system is actually the closest thing to a regular trial in the corporate system. It is, in a way, fairer to the terminated employee than the open-door appeal system. That system has been set up with the company's convenience in mind. The way it works is to management's advantage.

In the arbitration setup, on the other hand, the key to objectivity is in the makeup of the board of judges: management and employee representatives neutralize each other's advantage, with two on each side.

Oddly enough, such an arbitration system usually finds for management as often as it finds for the employee!

Using an Outside Arbitrator

The American Arbitration Association is an organization that has worked for years with arbitration experts. Through its auspices, a company can request an arbitrator from the organization to hear any appeal for reinstatement after termination, providing certain requirements are met.

The arbitrator holds a hearing at the company and then makes a ruling either for or against the grievant. The employer pays all the expenses of the arbitration.

The AAA has set up rules to be used in a case of arbitration in which one of its members appears. These are called Expedited Employment Rules; the guidelines establish the ground rules for employee-employer arbitration.

The use of the outside arbitrator is the last recourse for a terminated employee in an unsettled confrontation between himself or herself and an employer—that is, barring the court system.

By the time the arbitrator appears, the case has usually proceeded through all the basic steps of grievance mentioned above, plus the termination appeal. Then, once the termination appeal has been decided against the employee, he or she can still request the company to call in the American Arbitration Association to settle the case. The arbitrator, chosen by the AAA, usually works through the personnel department of the company.

How Arbitration Works

At a typical arbitration hearing, the employee is allowed one representative from within the company to appear on his or her behalf. When legal complications arise, the employee may be allowed to have an attorney present for representation.

The hearing itself tends to be more or less informal, although formal rules—"expedited" rules—are used to speed up the proceedings.

The employer may or may not choose to be bound by the arbitrator's rulings. So, too, may the employee choose to be or not be so bound.

Note: If the case continues past arbitration, it will move into the court system. There, the ruling of the arbitrator will carry more weight than the ruling of the company.

In deciding a case of termination, the arbitrator may not be allowed to rule for reinstatement but simply for financial compensation. Such rules are set up in advance of arbitration.

The difference between in-house arbitration and outside arbitration is the difference between the wide experience of the outside arbitrator and the probably more limited experience of the company arbitrator. For the employer or supervisor who is involved in the situation, the in-house arbitrator will probably be more sympathetic to the company cause. Nevertheless, the outside arbitrator *does* have total objectivity and noninvolvement—an advantage for him or her as well as for both contenders.

Informal or Formal System of Appeals?

Although there is no set rule for deciding whether to establish an informal or a formal system of appeal, it is usually true that for a smaller company a more informal system might work better. It would be an easy matter for a small firm to set up an open-door policy—as easy as it would be difficult for a large firm to initiate such a policy. As for the ombudsman approach, quite probably a medium-size company would be the most satisfactory place for such a system.

Many big companies have already set up some kind of appeal system, usually of a formal nature, with a progressive discipline system either built into it or used as a model alongside it.

The Personnel Department's Role in Termination

In a company with a personnel department, both hirings and firings, it would seem, should be primary departmental functions. Oddly enough, such is not usually the case. Most corporate personnel departments handle terminations in an indirect way. It is not too hard to understand why. One personnel manager explains: "Our job is to advise and counsel our managers on termination. We want to be sure that all supervisors apply procedures of termination consistently and objectively."

The personnel department does serve an ancillary function in termination. It keeps the evaluation records and the disciplinary sheets up to date. It also assembles an employee's file, including financial packages. It does not, however, set itself up as an impartial "court" to afford an opportunity for all employees to appeal a decision to terminate.

The reason?

Many personnel directors feel that the ability to terminate at will rests unequivocally with the supervisors of the various departments. Tampering with that prerogative is tantamount to destroying the authority of the manager/supervisor.

The Increase in Discrimination Charges

Certain firms are now beginning to set up appeal machinery within the personnel department to hear cases of nonunion employees who feel that they have been terminated unjustly.

"We had to do something," one personnel manager reports. "There's such an increase in the number of discrimination charges these days—sex, age, race—that it's too explosive a problem to try to bury within the corporate system. It's a whole new ball game."

The personnel department is the place where the employee's records are kept. For that reason it is an ideal spot to set up an appeal system. Not enough firms have yet inaugurated such systems. Discrimination challenges are not going to disappear. They will be more numerous in the future. The personnel department may be a good place for management to start cleaning house and to establish protection from extremely costly and damaging lawsuits.

Final Appeal in the Court System.

The use of an outside arbitrator may not signal the end of the controversy in a termination that a former employee regards as unjust. If the terminated still wants to fight the case, for whatever reason, he or she can go to the courts for a final hearing.

Unless the elements of the case are covered by specific statutes—discrimination by sex, age, race, or disability—or by ongoing public policy precedents, the employee may have to plead for a hearing. If the plea is deemed worthy, the case will then be tried in the courts.

In civil law there are two types of cases: torts and breaches of contract. A termination case is technically called a tort. In the tort the offense consists of the violation of some "duty" wholly set by law or by interpretation of law. That duty is an obligation imposed on all persons equally, and when that duty is breached, the injured party has the right to bring suit for compensatory damages.

In this type of tort, the terminated employee becomes the "plaintiff," and the terminator becomes the "defendant." The plaintiff must establish to the court's satisfaction a demonstrable breach of duty or an issue that can be used to seek damages from the defendant.

Note: Chapter 9 briefly studies certain termination cases in which laws have been broken and implied duties and obligations ignored or breached by terminators. A careful study of these types of legal cases should give the terminator a fair idea of what kinds of challenges can be expected from former employees who feel that they have been unjustly fired.

Summary

Termination may not be the end of the matter of discharge after all:

- Many firms have personnel departments that offer discharged employees a chance to plead for reinstatement or reassignment.
- Others having "human resources" departments may operate built-in appeal systems that can help reassign a terminated employee.
- Even the open-door policy may allow a discharged employee to have a hearing.

- Certain companies use ombudsmen as authoritarian figures to settle appeals.
- Others retool grievance machinery to handle cases of discharged employees seeking redress and reassignment.
- A growing number of firms now call in professional arbitrators to handle appeals in an objective fashion.
- When none of these systems provides a disgruntled terminatee with a satisfactory solution to his or her problem, the employee can justice always seek in the courts under tort law.

CHAPTER 9

Discrimination and the Courts

A MANAGER involved in any kind of termination action in an American company must always keep in mind the fact that a dismissal that affects anyone in four major groups of workers—plus a number of other workers who fall into certain categories because of their actions—must be considered as a possible adversary in court if the termination is not handled with surgical precision and delicacy.

The four groups—and rather large groups they are!—are these:

- Women, who may not be discriminated against because of their sex.
- Members of minority groups, who may not be discriminated against because of national origin or race.
- Workers over the age of forty, who may not be discriminated against because of their age.
- Disabled individuals, who may not be discriminated against because of their disabilities.

Those workers who fall into certain categories because of their actions include those who have become involved in "public policy" activities, are able to cite "implied contract violations," or have charged "malicious" or "unfair" termination.

The first four groups are covered by specific statutes. The other groups are covered by specific court precedents, although there are no laws directly concerned with their situations. Anyone falling into these protected categories may be able to sue charging discriminatory termination!

Termination at Will—How It Works

In order to understand why it was necessary for the courts to extend protection to certain groups of workers, let's take a brief look at the manner in which employers and employees have interacted with one another through the years.

From the time of the industrial revolution, it has been the standard practice of employers in the western world to hire employees at will and fire them at will. The concept, imbedded solidly as it was in English common law, came to America from across the sea with the Pilgrims when they landed. Not only that, but in America particularly the employee has always been—and still is—entitled to work at will and to leave the job at will. For many years, no one ever tried to change the concept.

Common law quite simply states that an employer has the absolute right to discharge an employee for whatever cause without incurring liability. It was not always exactly like that. During the years when industrial capitalism was in its infancy, an employer usually hired an employee with the tacit understanding that the arrangement was to remain in effect for at least a year. Then, at the end of the year, the employer or employee could terminate the obligation, the one to pay and the other to work. In special cases, if both parties agreed, a person could be hired for less than a year.

Today South Dakota still has a statute stipulating that a "hiring at a yearly rate is presumed to be for one year" and requires the employer to prove that there were sufficient grounds for termination before the end of a year.

Even so, it soon became the practice for both employer and employee to issue "reasonable notice" before a coming termination. Even that stipulation eventually began to erode in importance as the country continued to grow.

"For Good Cause, for No Cause . . ."

In 1884 the principle of termination at will was set down in the law books in a case tried in Tennessee, *Payne* v. *Western & A.R.R. Company.* Essentially, the point made in that case was that "all may dismiss their employees at will, be they many or few, for good cause, for no cause, or even for cause morally wrong without being thereby guilty of legal wrong." When asked to perform an illegal or unethical act in those days, an employee could either comply or quit the company.

That concept soon became a familiar one in other state courts throughout the country. The idea of termination at will confirmed the fact that the worker was not allowed to question a discharge by an employer. No one paying someone else to work was required to explain a sudden decision to discharge him or her. If the employer did not like the looks of the employee, that was reason enough for dismissal.

The relationship between employer and employee was in no way comparable to the relationship enjoyed today. It was, quite simply, that of "master and servant." A New York court put it this way: "The most fundamental rule of the law of master and servant is that which recognizes that, absent any applicable statutory or contractual provision to the contrary, an employer enjoys absolute power of dismissing his employee, with or without cause."

A Relationship of Mutuality

Supposedly, the idea of termination at will was equitable because of the "mutuality" of the concept. If the employee could quit at any time, then the employer should be able to terminate at any time, too. This specious logic ignored the fact that the employee always had the most to lose either in termination or in resignation—each having serious economic, psychological, and social consequences. Yet the impact of any resignation upon the day-to-day operation of a business organization was minimal. Mutuality? Hardly.

Still the United States Supreme Court in 1908, in *Adair* v. *United States*, put the burden of the relationship on the employee: "The right of the employee to quit the service of the employer, for whatever reason, is the same as the right of the employer, for whatever reason, to dispense with the services of such employee." In an opinion that would raise eyebrows today, the court pointed out that for the law to force an employer to keep an employee on against his or her will would be "slavery."

The master and servant relationship, with its fictional equitability, was upheld as late as 1974 by the United States Supreme Court in the *Geary* v. *U.S. Steel Corporation* decision. The ruling stated that "either party could terminate an employment relationship for any or no reason."

To date no federal or state statutes have been enacted specifically to override the common law doctrine of employment at will. But there have been advances toward that end.

The Big 1935 Breakthrough

The first milestone came with the passage of the Wagner Act of 1935. This statute prohibited employers from firing workers because of membership in a union or for activities in a union. Employees dismissed in violation of the law had the right to reinstatement with back pay. This was a breakthrough—a statute that gave the employee equal footing with the employer, even favoring the employee somewhat over the employer.

Once unions were recognized and allowed to make contracts with management, the union employee was protected by contract from "termination at will" as it had been practiced for years. Contractual agreements accepted as fundamental the right of employees to hold their jobs and not be terminated except for "just cause." That concept went directly against common law. Collective agreements under the National Labor Relations Act soon prohibited arbitrary discipline and dismissal of union members.

New Protective Statutes

On the heels of statutes to protect union members, other segments of the working population gradually earned protection from termination at will by the enactment of new laws.

One was the so-called sex discrimination act passed as part of the Equal Pay Act of 1963, which was in fact an amendment to the Fair Labor Standards Act of 1938. This was a law passed to prevent discrimination in employment because of sex. However, the standards usually considered and the rules and regulations consulted are all part of Title VII of the Civil Rights Act of 1964, passed a year afterward. This latter act primarily covered the rights of minorities.

We'll take these in two parts: first the sex discrimination act passed in 1963 and then the minority rights in employment act passed in 1964.

Equal Pay Act of 1963

The basic problem in sex discrimination is often not caused by prejudice against women in the work force, although it might *seem* to be, but by the age-old tradition ingrained in men of "protecting" women. The vision of the knight in shining armor riding forth to protect the fair maiden dies hard.

Lately, more astute observers of the employment scene have realized that such "protection" may really disguise a covert effort to keep women in the kitchen and out of the work place.

The plea for "equality" always runs into the stumbling block of childbirth and the consequent loss of work time involved in hospital admittance and subsequent child care. However, Title

VII of the Civil Rights Act has clarified pregnancy rights. They are covered in detail further on.

The Problem of the Double Standard

Many of the legal entanglements concerning discriminatory acts against female employees occur because of the fact that society in general has a preconceived and sometimes impractical notion about female conduct. What causes a certain action to be discriminatory may be the fact that males and females are treated unequally by society.

It is because of this double standard that Title VII of the Civil Rights Act spends so much time interpreting the proper conduct of male *and* female in the business world. Treating males and females differently is in direct violation of the precepts of Title VII, which say that *only one standard* shall apply to all cases under its purview—male and female.

A study of early court cases involving sex discrimination demonstrates one key point: *Any* standard set up by a firm must be imposed on females and males alike.

The problem surfaces when the first female employee is awarded a job that has never before been performed by a woman. If she cannot do the job according to the standard required, her superior, fearful of being accused of discrimination if he or she *removes* her from the job, may decide to make an accommodation for her inability. If the job requires lifting packing crates, for example, the employer may allow her to be helped by someone else.

Such accommodation, which is *not* required under Title VII, can cause trouble. If a compromise in job rules is permitted for a female employee, that same accommodation must also apply to all male employees. It is this point, and its ancillary complications, that causes the most perplexing trouble for management.

The Problem of Standards of Appearance

Society's long-standing double standard of conduct for men and women is the cause of a particularly disturbing type of lawsuit. It is based on business's "dress codes" or, as they are sometimes called, "appearance standards."

How can all rules apply equally to both male and female?

Answer: They can't. There are usually *two* standards rather than the one required by Title VII of the Civil Rights Act. Many court decisions have already pointed up the discrepancies and complications. For example:

- An employer can require a male to keep his hair at a certain length while having no requirements for the female employee.
- An employer's rule prohibiting a female employee from wearing pants in the executive office is *not* considered sexually discriminatory.
- However, in another case, the court says it *is* discriminatory to have a dress policy that requires female employees to wear "career ensembles" and permits male employees to wear business suits. Reason: The dress code for the female employees is "demeaning" to women because the career ensemble is considered a "uniform," and persons in uniform are usually subordinate to persons who are not. However, the court pointed out that a dress code requiring suits for males and females would *not* be considered a violation of Title VII.
- One employer requires male employees to wear ties but allows female employees to dress without ties, such a requirement being considered nondiscriminatory.
- A dress code for an airline cannot prohibit female cabin attendants from wearing glasses it if allows male employees to wear them.

Standards for Handling Pregnancy

Although it is difficult to picture both male and female being treated equally in regard to pregnancy, Title VII of the Civil Rights Act does set up certain standards of treatment for maternity.

To begin with, the law recognizes six different stages of pregnancy:

1. Conception.
2. The period of pregnancy when the female employee's ability to work is not affected.
3. The period of gestation during which the female employee's ability to work is affected.
4. Birth.

5. The period after delivery or miscarriage when the female employee is still physically unable to work.
6. The period involved with child rearing when the female employee is physically able to work but may desire to nurse and care for her child.

Pregnancy is a disability only during stages 3, 4, and 5. One important point for the employer of a female employee in the child rearing stage to note is that the law does not grant a leave of absence to a female after she has fully recovered from the delivery and is able to work. In fact, it is discriminatory for an employer to grant such a leave of absence unless the employer grants a *similar* leave of absence to its male employees who have fathered children!

There is also no legal requirement to permit a female to accrue seniority during the period of her disability caused by pregnancy unless the employer permits other employees, male and female, to accrue seniority during periods of disability of any kind.

If an employer permits a female employee who has had a child to maintain seniority and return to work at any time up to five years after the birth of a child, the employer may likewise be required to grant this allowance to any employee suffering a disability other than pregnancy.

Usually, an employer cannot cause a female employee to discontinue work because of pregnancy. Certain airlines, which must maintain stringent standards for the safety of passengers, can force pregnant employees to discontinue work, but these cases are considered unique.

And finally, an employer cannot force a mother to remain out of work for a set period of time after the delivery of her child.

In case history number 3, that of Monica Henry, it will be remembered that Don Riley did not bother to check out the background of his employee. The fact that she was a woman, and thus protected under Title VII of the Civil Rights Act, should have alerted him to the possibility of danger from legal action under statutory law.

In fact, it was not her protected position as a working woman that gave Monica Henry an edge but another facet of her background. Riley should not have blithely assumed that she would accept the age-old assumption that termination at will was sacrosanct. He was to be rudely awakened to his shortcomings as a terminator, as we shall soon see.

Civil Rights Act of 1964

The law that prohibits an employer from discriminating against an employee because of race, color, national origin, sex, or religion is Title VII of the Civil Rights Act of 1964. To enforce that law when it was passed by Congress, the Equal Employment Opportunity Commission (EEOC) was established in the same year.

Regulations of Title VII apply to such employers as federal, state, and local governments, schools, colleges, unions, and employment agencies. Employers included are those who hire fifteen or more employees for at least twenty calendar weeks in the year. There are a number of exemptions from the protection of Title VII:

- Religious institutions.
- Aliens.
- Members of the Communist Party.
- Persons elected to public office or appointed to the personal staff of persons elected to public office.

Note: The law does not protect persons who are not citizens of the United States from discrimination based upon their lack of citizenship. However, it does protect aliens from discrimination based upon their national origin.

Criteria for Proving Discrimination

A minority employee can usually sue an employer for discharge due to discrimination under Title VII if he or she can satisfactorily establish the following three points:

- The employee is a member of a minority group.
- Something "bad" has happened to the employee.
- "Something *else* unusual" exists in the termination history of the employee.

If these three criteria exist, and if the employee can prove all three to the satisfaction of the court, it is then up to the company to justify its actions in terminating the employee.

The crucial criterion, of course, is the third one: "something *else* unusual." The first two criteria are not really strong enough to establish a prima facie case of discrimination.

Here are several instances of how the "something else" criterion was applied to cases in litigation:

- In one case, the "something else" was simply the fact that the employee was one who had held the job for a number of years.
- In another case, the "something else" was merely the fact that the employee had no prior warning of the possible termination of the job.
- In still another, the "something else" was the fact that the employer had made no previous complaints before dismissal "for cause."
- In a fourth case, the "something else" was the fact that the employer did not follow the regular termination procedures of the company, even though the procedures were not in writing.

Note: The establishment of these three primary points in proving discrimination does not *automatically* win a case. However, it does put the burden on the employer to prove that the termination action was taken without discrimination because of race, color, national origin, sex, or religion.

Four Main Areas of Discrimination

The manager involved in terminating any employee must constantly keep in mind that there are four main areas of law under which the employee can claim discrimination in dismissal because of race, color, national origin, sex, or religion. These four areas—which by no means encompass all cases of discrimination—are dismissal because of

- "Characteristics of a minority group"
- "Too vague" work standards
- A "move to the suburbs"
- "Discriminatory seniority"

Characteristics of a Minority Group

If a member of a minority group can establish the fact that an employer considered any "characteristics of a minority group" in reaching a decision to terminate, the minority member can establish a case and may win it in court. This charge is one of the most common in bringing a case to court under Title VII.

A bus company for example, employed both blacks and whites as drivers. The company had a policy of using only clean-shaven employees in driving jobs. It was considered a good image-making policy and excellent public relations. When one black driver insisted on wearing a beard on the job, he was called on the carpet and told to shave it off. He refused. When he persisted in appearing on the job in a beard, he was given another order and then terminated.

The employee took the company to court, where it was determined that he had a skin condition called pseudo-folliculitis barbae, a problem common among black males. It causes hair follicles to curl back into the skin after shaving, producing inflammation. The employee pointed out that he had been told by his doctor to grow a beard to prevent a worsening of the problem.

The court determined that the no-beard rule was distinct discrimination against black males and, hence, against the terminated employee. He got his job again with full back pay.

"Too Vague" Work Standards

Another argument that can be used by a minority employee to challenge a dismissal is that of work standards that are "too vague" to be applied to everyone. If such a "vague standard" can be proved to have been used by an employer as grounds for terminating a minority employee, such a termination may be judged unjustified.

A "Move to the Suburbs"

One argument that has been effective in court for proving discrimination against minorities is that of a specific "move to the suburbs" by a company or corporation. When such a move is made, a great many employees who are members of minorities are left behind in the urban center from which the company has departed. The move thus causes the work force to suffer a net loss of minority employees.

Discriminatory Seniority

One of the most troublesome areas in cases of termination involves minorities dismissed according to a seniority system that has been set up by a company in order to protect its more permanent employees.

Members of minority groups usually claim that a seniority system itself discriminates against them because in general they have been hired or promoted in greater numbers *more recently* than employees who are not members of minority groups.

In most cases, the employer follows the seniority system anyway—that is, last hired, first fired. Many court cases have justified layoffs if the seniority system can be proved to be an honest one.

The courts usually follow the principles involved in collective-bargaining agreements formed between employers and unions:

- It is permissible to terminate according to a seniority system even though the end result may be the termination of a larger number of minority employees than nonminority employees. This presumes that the seniority system must have been set up as a bona fide system and not created especially for the purpose of segregating males from females, blacks from whites, and so on.
- Such a system of seniority does not have to be rigidly adhered to in line of progression and in each department. The general rule is that employees are entitled to what is called "constructive seniority" if they can prove that they would have had earlier seniority except for discriminatory acts of an employer and/or a union. Such a "constructive" date is the date the employee would have been in line of progression had it not been for the act of discrimination. The usual reduction in force causes employees to be laid off according to seniority, but for those who have "constructive seniority," *that* date is the one that counts.
- To achieve a "constructive seniority" date, the employee involved must file a charge of discrimination with EEOC or be a member of a class whose representative has filed a charge

with EEOC within 180 days of the allegedly discriminatory action.

In spite of the three principles discussed above, an employer who uses a seniority system to reduce the work force can always be called to trial by EEOC. No seniority system is sacrosanct. In one of its decisions, EEOC ruled that the use of a seniority system as the only basis for terminations might violate Title VII. The rationale for this decision is that if there was past discrimination against minorities that kept them out of an employment system and made them unable to achieve as much seniority as nonminorities, the use of seniority as a basis for termination violates Title VII.

Take the case of Monica Henry in chapter 1. After she was terminated by Don Riley, she went out to look for another job. Things had changed from the year before. Companies were not hiring now. There had been a fluctuation in the economy. In her interviews she met another woman who was also looking for a job. In their ensuing conversations, Monica Henry learned that she might have grounds for a discrimination suit against Atlas Industries for the way she had been fired.

Although her name was Henry and she did not look any different from millions of other Americans, she had been born in Puerto Rico. After moving to New York as a teenager, she had lost most of her accent. She had then gone to school to learn secretarial skills. Her spelling and grammar were still shaky when she was hired by Atlas Industries.

She learned that because she was Puerto Rican, and therefore a member of a minority group in the eyes of the law, she was protected by Title VII of the Civil Rights Act. Don Riley had not actually fired her *because* she was Puerto Rican; he had not even *known* of her origins. He had fired her because she was the last one hired and because she was slow at her secretarial work.

Monica Henry nevertheless got a lawyer to represent her and appeared in court to demonstrate that Atlas Industries had fired her in a discriminatory fashion.

First of all, she proved with no trouble at all that she was of Puerto Rican birth and therefore a member of a minority group.

Second, she proved that "something bad" had happened to her—specifically, that she had been terminated.

Third, she proved that "something else unusual" had happened to her—specifically, that she had been terminated for "unsatisfactory performance" even though her employer had never complained to her about her work.

Don Riley was required to tell why he had terminated Monica Henry without warning her that her performance was not up to standard. Riley explained that he had not terminated her *only* because of her performance but because she was the obvious one to go in light of general seniority rules—last in first out.

When questioned on the point of Monica Henry's "unsatisfactory" job performance, Don Riley admitted that he had no evaluation records to prove that her work was not entirely satisfactory.

That was enough for the court. Monica Henry was awarded damages and pay for the period between her termination and the court finding and was also reinstated.

Age Discrimination in Employment Act of 1967

Another statute for the manager involved in terminations to be cognizant of is that which prevents discrimination against an employee because of age. Originally passed in 1967 and usually referred to as "ADEA," the Age Discrimination in Employment Act was amended and brought up to date in 1978.

The act states quite unequivocally that it is illegal for an employer to discharge any employee "because of the individual's age."

Primarily, the statute covers anyone between the ages of forty and seventy years, applying equally to employers, labor organizations, employment agencies, the federal government, and state governments.

It is limited to employers that have work forces of twenty or more employees and hire them for twenty or more calendar weeks of the year. It is also limited to labor organizations that have over twenty-five members. It applies equally to hiring, to assigning, to training, to promoting, and to terms and conditions of employment.

Under the ADEA statutes certain employees have been able to prove that while age was not actually the specific reason for their termination, the real reason was *related* to age and was for that reason a violation of the law.

In one case, an employer tried to terminate all fire fighters who were sixty-two years of age or older. There was, according to the employer, a greater risk of injury not only to fire fighters of that age but also to those they were trying to help.

Several of the terminated fire fighters decided to fight for their jobs. They insisted that they were *not* less effective than their co-workers. Why, for example, was sixty-two the magic age? Did they suddenly become less effective on their sixty-second birthday?

Their arguments made good sense to the courts. When the case was heard, the ruling was in their favor. It was determined that the standard that had been imposed was based on an arbitrary age stipulation rather than on their health, ability, and training. Thus, it was discriminatory and, because discriminatory, illegal.

How to Handle Cases of Age Discrimination

In spite of the disadvantage the average employer encounters in fighting court cases on age discrimination charges, dismissals *have* been upheld against certain claims. Judgments went to employers who were able to demonstrate that termination was due not to age but to the following:

- Unsatisfactory work performance.
- Tardiness.
- Loss of business.
- Higher labor costs involved in keeping an employee who happened to be older.
- Abolishing of the position in question, even though other employees assumed some of the worker's duties.
- A requirement, dictated by sound business judgment, that a group of people be terminated.

Use of Labor Costs in Planning a Termination

An employer can consider the cost of labor when planning whom to terminate. However, if the employer should act under the general principle that any older worker is going to be earning more money than a younger worker—because of higher medical costs, significant pension contributions, or the greater likelihood of suffering debilitating injury than a younger person—that employer might find itself trapped. Labor costs must be considered on an individualized basis, *not* on a class basis; otherwise, a termination action can be considered a violation of ADEA.

Considering Percentages of Older Employees Terminated

When contemplating any reduction in force, it is advantageous for the employer to keep ADEA violations in mind. For example, the employer should review the impact of all terminations on the various age groups within the 40-plus area. That is, the employer must consider the percentage of employees schedule for dismissal who are between 40 and 45, 45 and 50, 50 and 55, 55 and 60, and 60 and 70.

If the figures show a net reduction in the average age of the remaining work force, plus a more significant adverse impact against workers in the older age ranges, discrimination may be easy to prove.

Back in case history number 1, when Don Riley terminated Randy White, he had no idea that White might accuse him later of violating ADEA. However, some months after White's termination, he developed such a passionate animosity toward everyone and everything at Atlas Industries that he decided to do something about it. He considered himself monumentally put upon. In discussions with people he knew in other companies, he constantly excoriated the firm for its actions in firing him.

Eventually he began to attribute imagined motivations to Riley and top management at Atlas. It grew in his mind that he had been fired because he was getting too old to do the job. After all, Riley had told him that he hadn't really been performing "up to par." Didn't that mean that he was getting old? What else but old age would cause his performance to slump?

Two months after his termination, Atlas Industries hired a replacement for White. Through the grapevine White learned that the new assistant marketing director was a thirty-five-year-old "hotshot" from a rival firm. Had they fingered White's replacement *before* they got rid of him?

At a cocktail party White was chatting with a college friend who had become a corporate lawyer. He mentioned his replacement, describing him as a "young punk."

"How young?" the lawyer asked.

White told him.

"You've got them," laughed his friend. And he went on to explain why.

Within weeks White was in court, suing Atlas Industries for discriminatory termination because of age. White's main point—as suggested by his lawyer friend—was that he had been fired only because of his age, which was forty-five. Proof of that was the fact that he had been replaced by a thirty-five-year-old employee. Why else would there be an age difference of ten years?

In court Riley tried to point out that he had terminated White because of bad performance due to corporate burnout—but since he had no records to back up his claim to that effect, the judge would not accept that as fact. Atlas lost the case, and White won a considerable sum in damages.

In the termination of Jim Young, case history number 4, Mark Andrews was well aware of Young's age and the fact that Young might be able to claim illegal termination under ADEA. To forestall any such charge, the company planned not to hire anyone to replace him in his position but rather to abandon the position. Taking on a younger person to fill the same position would have given the courts a distinct impression that age did have something to do with Young's termination.

Rehabilitation Act of 1973

Another statute that any manager involved in terminations must always keep in mind is that dealing with handicapped or disabled persons. The Rehabilitation Act of 1973 protects all such employees who are not covered by union contracts or who are not included under age, race, or sex discrimination laws.

A "handicapped" person is defined by the statute as being a person who has a physical or mental impairment that limits one or more major life activities, who has a record of such an impairment, or who is regarded by others as having such an impairment.

The Office of Federal Contract Compliance Programs was designated by Congress to enforce the laws included in the Rehabilitation Act of 1973. In the early years of the act's existence, OFCCP decided that alcoholism and drug abuse were "handicaps," as well as blindness, deafness, and other conditions more generally recognized as handicaps.

After conflict between OFCCP and the government, Congress amended the Rehabilitation Act explicitly to remove alcoholism and drug abuse from protection by the statute. The amendment became effective in 1978.

Who Is Covered by the Statute?

The definition of "handicap" is still being extended from its original scope. Epilepsy and even obesity are sometimes considered handicaps; so were alcoholism and drug abuse until Congress stepped in. Nevertheless, certain cases of alcoholism and drug abuse are argued in state courts, where both are considered handicaps in the legal sense. A fuller discussion follows.

The problem in determining true disability is one of definition. Trying to determine discrimination against a disabled person involves mostly trying to discover exactly what the disability is. Several areas of conflict exist in such a search.

Three Gray Areas

The first and most common area of conflict is in determining whether or not the disability, no matter what it consists of, is permanent or long-term or whether it is simply temporary.

The second gray area involves examining a condition that does not currently impair an employee's ability to perform but may very likely do so in the future. A factor in resolving this moot point is the establishment of a possibility that continued activity in the job may aggravate the condition, thus consciously condoning and adding to the disability.

A third arguable area is the burden of proof—that is, whether the employee has to prove that his or her condition will not affect work performance in order to be considered disabled or handicapped in a legal sense, or whether the employer has to prove the employee's inability to perform according to job specifications.

Long-Term Disability Versus Short-Term

In the first area—long-term versus short-term disability—the courts in Wisconsin have found asthma, migraine headaches, alcoholism, diabetes, a deviated septum, and rheumatoid arthritis to be handicaps covered by the statute. But Rhode Island requires the handicap to be "a serious injury or impairment of more than a temporary nature." In other words, a condition such as whiplash is *not* legally considered a handicap.

On a federal court level, the opinion seems to be that an employee who can perform most or many jobs does not suffer from a "substantial impairment" and is not considered handicapped. This opinion is still being argued in various courts.

The Ability to Perform Now Versus in the Future

In the second area, involving the ability to perform now but perhaps not in the future, certain states permit the employer to look ahead in time:

- In Oregon a court decided that an employer could terminate an employee because the worker's condition would increase a risk of incapacitation while performing the job.
- In Washington an employer was allowed to consider the employee's present ability to perform, the safety of that person and his or her co-workers, *and* future deterioration.
- In New York an employer was allowed to assume that a prospective employee suffering from dermatitis would be hurt by exposure to work and refuse to hire him.
- In Wisconsin, on the other hand, an employer could not refuse to hire a person even though performing the job might cause him or her to become incapacitated.

The Burden of Proof

In the third area, burden of proof in establishing disability, there are several conflicts:

- In New York a school bus driver with a hearing defect had quit his job before his hearing became impaired. When he tried to return to work, he was refused and he sued. The court found that his hearing disability was job-related—that is, it *would* affect his job performance. The point is that a disability, to constitute discrimination, must *not* affect job performance. The burden of proof concerning job worthiness is up to the employee.
- In Wisconsin the burden is on the employer to prove that a disabled employee cannot perform the job satisfactorily.

- A court in the state of Washington found that an employer discriminated against an employee who was afflicted with cerebral palsy by transferring him to a job that the company knew or should have known he could not perform.

Case Histories of Typical Disability Problems

Blindness, epilepsy, alcoholism, and drug abuse are featured in many typical case histories. For instance, a blind applicant was refused employment as a legal research analyst. The applicant would need a reader to work with him. A requirement for the job was sufficient visual acuity to enable the employee to read. That is, the physical requirement was validly job-related. The employer's refusal to hire was upheld.

In another case, a city government had a rule refusing to hire anyone who had experienced an epileptic seizure within the two years prior to the date of application. The law was struck down as discriminatory.

In case history number 5 in chapter 1, Mark Andrews had already studied the legal ramifications of Dick Barton's drug addiction and methadone maintenance program. He based his judgment that Barton would be unable to sue Maddon, Inc., on a complicated court case that had occurred in New York when the New York Transit Authority had refused to hire anyone who was on a methadone maintenance program for a motorman's job. The case was argued under the U.S. Constitution and Title VII, because the rule had the effect of screening out more blacks than whites. The court found the rule to be justified for business reasons. The point is that as long as an individual is on a maintenance program, he or she is not yet rehabilitated. Therefore, the individual cannot be considered protected by the Rehabilitation Act.

Asthma, heart murmur, and deafness are some of the other disabilities covered by the Rehabilitation Act of 1973. Protection is similar to that discussed above for blindness, epilepsy, and drug abuse.

The Dilemma about Alcoholism

In order to take any action at all against an employee for alcoholism, the employer has to prove that the condition affects the person's work performance. If, after such a determination, the employer does then terminate the employee, there is always the possibility that the worker can demand treatment for disability—that is, alcoholism—the same as any other person covered by the company's benefits program.

Since many disability benefits programs do not cover alcoholism as a disability, the employer may be required to make payments to the alcoholic out of pocket, without benefit of insurance coverage.

Note: In the 1978 amendment to the Rehabilitation Act of 1973, it is stated that a person with a drinking problem—whether that be defined as simply "a problem" or as "alcoholism"—is not protected by the Rehabilitation Act of 1973 if the condition affects his or her ability to perform the job or endangers the safety of others at work.

In spite of the extent of court protection for the groups just mentioned, there are federal and state laws that now protect groups like war veterans and public employees in civil service and government jobs from unjust dismissal. Teachers are protected under tenure laws, and often local governments provide ordinances regarding job security.

The "protected class" designation now covers a much larger segment of society, affording a safety net for literally millions of nonunion workers.

Coverage by Court Precedent

In spite of the extent of such protection, there were still millions of nonminority workers left unprotected—"majority" workers who were male, who were white, who were under forty, and who were prime targets for any kind of purge management might want to conduct. They were and still are sitting ducks.

The use of statutes to protect terminated employees alerted other unprotected "majority" workers to the position of the courts, which now seemed tilted toward helping employee against employer, quite contrary to tradition. Soon individual employees, terminated for reasons that smacked of favoritism, of malice, of "unjust cause," began to sue for reinstatement and damages.

Even without statutes to protect them, scores of individuals managed to win cases involving termination that could be shown to be "unjust" or "unfair." These cases fell roughly into three basic categories: "public policy" firings, "implied" firings, and "malicious termination" firings.

Considerations of "Public Policy"

Briefly, public policy cases involve terminations motivated by actions an employee might take in the public interest against the company employing him or her. If the employee could prove that the discharge violated a clear public policy of the state, enunciated by the state constitution, statutes, regulations, or decisional law, he or she could sue to have the discharge set aside.

The popular term *whistle-blowing* became linked to this type of case, but some public policy cases involved the employee's refusal to participate in illegal acts, insistence upon serving on a jury, or signing up for military service.

In determining such a case, ancillary considerations such as motive for discharge, verbal employment assurances, the extent to which public issues are involved, public safety regulations, judicial processes, and even the disposition of the particular courts in which a grievance can be heard become important issues.

For the employer contemplating a specific termination, all these factors, as well as the discriminatory issues discussed in the preceding section, become of primary significance in determining procedure and manner.

The original concept of employment at will—the slave and master concept—held that the employee was required to do whatever the employer told him or her to do or risk being terminated for disobedience. Later on, the concept altered slightly so that the master/slave relationship became a bit less pronounced. Still, the employee was required to carry out the employer's orders or risk forfeiture of pay or termination.

The concept for many years resembled the relationship in the armed forces between enlisted man and officer, eventually running up the chain of command to the top man—the commander-in-chief. During wartime the enlisted man has a mandate to kill the enemy. Such a mandate violates the biblical commandment: Thou shalt not kill. Nevertheless, because of the nature of the relationship, based as it is on the destruction of the enemy and the survival of the allies, the moral right and wrong of a soldier's action is unquestioned within the parameters of duty.

In recent military operations—Vietnam, for example—certain enlisted men were able to mitigate charges of disobedience by demonstrating that the orders given them by their superiors were suicidal, demented, or detrimental to the service itself. Although these citations were not called "public policy considerations," they were not far from it.

As used today, the phrase *public policy* usually concerns a simple but basic conflict of desires. Management desires one thing; an employee's desire runs counter to management's. The result is the employee's refusal to obey orders. Termination for cause—disobedience—follows. A court case results in which the court may come out on the side of the employee if the action was judged to have been taken "in the public interest" or "in the interest of truth, justice, or right."

An Early Public Policy Case

One of the earliest public policy cases occurred in 1959. Because the decision paved the way for the use of public policy as a consideration in a case of wrongful termination, it became a landmark decision.

The employee involved was a business agent hired by a large trade union. He was called to testify before a legislative committee investigating wrongdoing in trade unionism. Before appearing, he was called in by his own superior and given instructions on how to respond to certain questions. The employee knew that these answers were false.

Once on the stand, the employee opted to tell the truth, as required by the oath he had taken. In deciding to tell the truth, he disobeyed the instructions given him by his superior. When the union learned what had happened, he was fired for refusing to follow the orders he had been given.

The employee sued, claiming that he had been instructed to do something that clearly violated the law—namely, to commit perjury, a criminal offense—and that when he had refused to lie, the union had terminated him.

The point was that the employee had been given a Hobson's

choice. No matter what he did, he would be doing wrong: violating criminal law on the one hand or violating an employer's direct orders on the other. He had chosen to obey a directive that had higher priority—criminal law as opposed to an employer's orders.

The court, deciding that the employee had acted correctly, ordered him reinstated. It also concluded that as a matter of "public policy and sound morality," the employer's conduct could not be condoned. Here is part of the court's decision:

> The commission of perjury is unlawful. . . . It would be obnoxious to the interests of the state and contrary to public policy and sound morality to allow an employer to discharge any employee, whether the employment be for a designated or unspecified duration, on the ground that the employee declined to commit perjury, an act specifically enjoined by statute. . . . The public policy of this state . . . would be seriously impaired if it were to be held that one could be discharged by reason of his refusal to commit perjury. To hold that one's continued employment could be made contingent upon his commission of a felonious act at the instance of his employer would be to encourage criminal conduct upon the part of both the employee and employer and serve to contaminate the honest administration of public affairs.

Thus, even though no law prohibited the discharge of a worker on such grounds, the fundamental principles of public policy and the adherence to the objective underlying the state's penal statutes require the recognition of a rule barring an employer from discharging an employee who has simply complied with his or her legal duty and has refused to comit an illegal act.

The Case of the Honest Salesman

A similar case involved an employee who was hired by a petroleum corporation as a clerk and later rose to be retail sales representative. His duties in sales included liaison between the company and independent service station dealers in an assigned territory on the West Coast.

Some ten years after he started work, he found himself involved in a series of actions that he knew to be illegal. He took his orders from the district manager, who, he learned, was engaged in "reducing, controlling, stabilizing, fixing, and pegging the retail gasoline prices" of the service stations.

At first the employee complied with orders, believing it his duty to do so. However, as the pressure increased on him to force price reductions to undercut competition, thus causing the franchise operators running the stations to lose money unfairly, he complained to management.

The pressure let up for a while, but soon his supervisor repeated his original orders. This time the employee refused to go along with the scheme, which he said was "price-fixing" and therefore illegal. His supervisor threatened him with dismissal if he did not comply. He agreed to obey orders for a bit longer but finally refused to do so.

Within a few weeks he was fired. His discharge, according to the records, was for "incompetence" and for "unsatisfactory performance." The employee felt he was being fired for refusing to force prices down at the independent dealer stations.

He sued the company for termination based on his refusal to participate in an illegal scheme, the fixing of gasoline prices. He won his case. In its opinion, the court stated: "The days when a servant was practically the slave of his master have long since passed." In addition:

> We hold that an employer's authority over its employee does not include the right to demand that the employee commit a criminal act to further its interests, and an employer may not coerce compliance with such unlawful directions by discharging an employee who refuses to follow such an order. An employer engaging in such conduct violates a basic duty imposed by law upon all employers, and thus an employee who has suffered damages as a result of such discharge may maintain a tort action for wrongful discharge against the employer.

When the Whistle Blows

Public policy does not end with cases of direct conflict between the moral codes of employer and employee. The concept stretches further than that. If an employee believes that his or her employer is producing shoddy goods that might injure the public—and says so—the employee is certainly violating a traditional concept of obedience and fealty. If the employer terminates the employee for what he or she has said in public, it seems that the company is acting clearly with its rights under the old concept of termination at will.

But wait!

Whistle-blowing—the criticism of a product or of a producer of a product by a person engaged in manufacturing or merchandising that product—has become recognized by the courts as a bona fide extension of the public policy concept.

Whistle-Blowing about Public Safety

"Public safety" is a subject that now intrigues the courts much more than it did in the past. Combined with whistle-blowing, a public safety consideration can usually produce a courtroom response favorable to the employee.

The classic public safety case involved three engineers who were fired from their jobs after complaining that the work in progress on a massive transportation system in a large American city did not offer proper safeguards against accidents. The terminations took place during the construction of the line.

One of the employees was a computer systems engineer, and the other two were electronics construction engineers. They were involved in designing and testing the equipment. They found malfunctions in the signal reception equipment, which was made by an outside firm of national reputation. They urged delay in accepting the system until the bugs were worked out. However, the construction deadline had already passed; the general manager did not want any more postponements.

The three engineers eventually confronted the general manager head-on. Direct orders were given to fudge reports of tests. Some of the orders were obeyed.

However, the three engineers eventually had enough and decided that they would have to stand up to management for the sake of public safety, which was in their hands. They refused to go along with any more "massaged" test reports. Their refusal set off a triple termination, with the general manager ordering it.

Later the engineers revealed their story to the press. Various engineering associations investigated. Three years after their termination, the three engineers sued the transportation company. Before the case went to trial, the firm made an out-of-court settlement in the amount of seventy-five thousand dollars.

In this case, many details of which have been omitted here for reasons of space, the key element of the conflict was the fact that the company's management considered an engineer on the same level as a clerk or secretary—that is, a mechanic rather than a planner and thinker. The facts were otherwise. The controversy would never have been allowed to assume the proportions it did had the general manager been an engineer or been trained in electronics.

The story of Arthur Mason in case history number 2 in Chapter 1 is a whistle-blowing case. It will be remembered that when Don Riley was terminating him, Mason hinted at the possibility that Riley's motive in the dismissal might have been Mason's earlier criticism of an airplane valve made by Atlas Industries.

After his termination, Mason brooded some time about his treatment at the hands of Don Riley. He knew Riley disliked him, and he knew he had been a thorn in the side of management from the moment he had been hired. He suspected, as he had intimated to Riley, that Atlas was firing him because of his whistle-blowing activities in connection with the suspect valve.

He decided to sue for discriminatory termination as a whistle-blower critical of a faulty Atlas product. Until Riley terminated Mason, he had utterly forgotten Mason's part in the bad publicity about the airplane valve. However, Atlas had ceased making the valve after Mason had blown the whistle on it and had issued a substitute with a completely modified design. It was a tacit admission that Mason's criticism was substantially correct. Riley, who paid little attention to such details, did not even know of the change.

During the trial against Atlas, Mason produced witnesses to the fact that he had spoken about the valve to management, that the information had at first been ignored, that he had written a letter that was published in the newspaper, and that his criticism was factually correct, inasmuch as the design had been radically modified afterward.

Riley countered with the story of Mason's sorry performance as well as with witnesses who testified that Mason had been involved in fights with other employees, attesting to his "uncooperative attitude" on the work scene. But Riley could not substantiate the poor job performance charge because the company kept no records or evaluation charts.

The court found for Mason and awarded him damages. The point was that the whistle-blowing incident, completely documented and satisfactorily proved to the court by Mason, was enough to imply that Atlas Industries had indeed terminated Mason not because of poor performance (totally undocumented) but because of his anticorporate whistle-blowing activities.

A List of Public Policy States

States that prohibit termination for refusing to commit perjury, for filing workers' compensation or other state-sanctioned claims, for refusing to perform sexual acts, or for blowing the whistle on unsafe or defective products are: California, Connecticut, Idaho, Illinois, Indiana, Kansas, Maryland, Massachusetts, Michigan, Missouri, Montana, New Hampshire, New Jersey, New York, Oregon, Pennsylvania, Texas, Washington, and West Virginia.

The following *might* do so under certain circumstances: Alabama, Colorado, District of Columbia, Iowa, Mississippi, and Vermont.

Considerations of the "Implied Contract"

What one observer described as a "most unexpected development in the law of unfair dismissal" has recently occurred in cases of "implied cntract" between company and employee. Typically, when he or she is hired, an employee does not enter into a written contract with an employer. There are exceptions—high-echelon management positions or high-paying work areas such as the entertainment business or the sports world.

For the average worker, however, no contract is drawn up at the time of hiring. In recent years the courts have begun to feel that in spite of the absence of documentary evidence, an implied contract has been negotiated that is sealed with the employer's words: "You're hired." The employer, in agreeing to pay wages or salary to an employee, in effect enters into an unstated contract with the employee; it is an agreement that must be honored.

If an employee can prove in court that at the time of hiring, such an implied agreement contained a particular proviso—for example, to the effect that the employee would continue working indefinitely and be dismissed *only* for a specific cause—the company then could not terminate except for a satisfactory and irreproachable reason. If the implied contract can be shown to have been violated, the employer is liable for reinstatement and/or damages.

Such an implied contract can be verbal, expressed at the time of the interview, or it can be in the form of a manual or brochure explaining the rules and regulations of the company. If the manual states that discharge can occur only for specific reasons, those reasons and those reasons alone can be used by the company for dismissal of the employee. If the agreement is verbal and has been witnessed, that, too, can constitute proof of contract for the courts.

"As Long as He Did His Job"

An employee in a midwestern health insurance company was handed documents at the time he was hired stating that he would not be dismissed except "for just cause only." The documents were actually the manual and guidelines of company policy pertaining to many subjects, including discipline and termination.

The employee was eventually fired for what he felt was not "just cause." He sued. In his testimony he stated that he had been told he would be with the company until mandatory retirement at age sixty-five "as long as I did my job." He could also point to the company manual that said he would be dismissed "for just cause only" and then only after specific disciplinary procedures were implemented—warning, hearing, and so on. When he was told to resign, the supervisory decision was reviewed by the personnel department, but the procedures outlined in the supervisory manual were not carried out.

The court determined that the employer "has established a company policy to discharge for just cause only, pursuant to certain procedures, had made that policy known to [the employee], and thereby had committed itself to discharge him only for just cause in compliance with the procedures."

Even though the company manual was not signed by both parties, the court determined that its statements held as contractual obligations:

> If there is in effect a policy to dismiss for cause only, the employer may not depart from that policy at whim simply because

he was under no obligation to institute the policy in the first place. Having announced the policy, presumably with a view of obtaining the benefit of improved employee attitudes and behavior and improved quality of the work force, the employer may not treat its promise as illusory.

The court determined that the employee had been fired in an arbitrary manner and not according to the rules and precepts enunciated in the company manual. He was awarded seventy-two thousand dollars in damages.

A promotion executive was hired by a large New York publishing firm and enjoyed excellent working relations for seven years. When he was hired, he had received a handbook on personnel policies, and in it a statement appeared that no employee would be dismissed for other than "just and sufficient cause."

Seven years after he was hired, he was suddenly dismissed. He was unable to appeal his case through company channels and sued. In court he claimed that he had been terminated in violation of the personnel policies stated in the company handbook.

The state court of appeals ruled that the handbook provision constituted a contract between employer and employee. It ordered the employee's case to be tried by a lower court.

The employee said later:

> I was very surprised by the firing. I worked there for seven years, and I didn't think they could just call me in and do that. They have an active program of informing people of the [company] code of ethics, a part of which is that people would be dismissed only after all other possible steps for curing the problem have been exhausted. I didn't even get any warning.

"A Situation Instinct with an Obligation"

Management cannot avoid implied responsibility by making a claim that a handbook or personnel brochure is simply a good "public relations" ploy used to try to attract workers to the company. One court ruling specifically points out that such an excuse is insufficient:

> If an employer chooses to create an environment in which the employee believes that, whatever the personnel procedures and practices, they are established and official at a given time, pur-

port to be fair, and are applied consistently and uniformly to each employee, it has created a situation instinct with an obligation.

How to Prevent Implied Contract Lawsuits

One manager of personnel administration for a large *Fortune* 500 company writes:

> Review your recruiting ad copy and brochures. One major firm recently ran a help-wanted ad in *The Wall Street Journal* promising that successful candidates would be *assured* a fast track career potential. If you want to make such unqualified statements, fine. . . . But be ready to back them up.
>
> Make sure your *future* personnel policy statements say what you mean. There is nothing wrong with "usually," "in most cases," or other qualifiers; they are not "weasel words." Using judgment and discretion is what managers get paid for. Employees—especially employee-managers—understand that. Frequently, a little such judgment serves the employee better than blind enforcement of rigid rules.
>
> When you have already made an unqualified statement that could be seen as a pledge to employees, think twice about changing or ignoring it. Regardless of what you may have meant to say, it is sometimes cheaper to bite the bullet than to risk getting shot.

One labor lawyer notes:

> If the manual says there's a probationary period after which the worker becomes a permanent employee, or even if the application form says there's a probationary period, that, too, could create an implied contract. I'm telling our clients that they should add some language to the effect of, "If hired, I understand I can leave at any time or can be fired at any time."

Another attorney engaged in employer-employee relations says: "[The situation] has very broad implications because employment manuals were written by personnel people to give employees comfort that they worked for a fair employer and perhaps without cognizance of the potential liability they were creating for their employers."

One health insurance company has already taken care of the problem in a hardheaded way: "We have changed our employee handbook so that it very explicitly states that you can be terminated at any time for any reason just as you can terminate at any time for any reason. It also says that it is not an employment contract."

Yet some attorneys feel that even that solution is fraught with problems. "If you begin your relationship with an employee by saying, 'We owe you nothing,' you know what kind of people you're going to have working for you? They're going to have absolutely no institutional loyalty."

A List of Implied Contract States

States that prohibit termination in violation of an implied contract are: California, Connecticut, Idaho, Louisiana, Maine, Massachusetts, Michigan, Montana, Nebraska, New Hampshire, North Carolina, and Oklahoma.

Considerations of "Malicious Termination"

Although a typical "whistle-blowing" termination might easily be called a "malicious" termination, there is a slight difference. There are cases of wrongful discharge that have nothing to do with blowing the whistle against a company.

The key element in this type of case is the word *malicious.* The type of complaint is also called a "tort of outrage." (As has been explained, the kind of case involved in all termination court proceedings is a "tort"—an argument of one person against another in a noncriminal sense.)

Although there is no limit to the situations that can arise in this type of case, most of them follow a pattern that is similar to the public policy and implied contract cases. There are, however, even some cases involving invasion of employee privacy.

In one such instance, a woman began working as senior secretary to a large corporation's director of facilities planning when the company was contemplating a move of its corporate headquarters from one city to another. She was twenty-six, divorced and remarried. In the new community where the company was moving, she settled down in a comfortable job, with one upsetting complication.

Her immediate superior, the director of facilities planning, began a concerted effort to seduce her. Although she refused him, he continued his attentions, giving her good evaluation marks and promotions. He even told her he would establish her in a posh apartment if she would leave her husband and be his mistress.

On trips back to the original corporate headquarters, she found herself involved in various intimate situations with him. He would invite her to dinner but wind up in his hotel room with her; she would have to walk out. Once he instructed her to bring files to his hotel room; he let her in dressed in a bathrobe and sat her down at a breakfast for two.

This cat-and-mouse game lasted for three years. Finally he said that if she would not capitulate, he would fire her. By now she had been promoted to associate facilities planner. Nevertheless, within a month she was out of a job.

She sued and was awarded damages in the form of back pay and lost employment benefits.

In her confrontation with Mark Andrews, Mary Healy cited the possibility of "malicious termination" during case history number 6. But Andrews had read his employee correctly and had gathered all the pertinent information needed to prove management's side in the courts.

However, he knew he was on shaky ground when it came to her threat to accuse him falsely of retaliation against her for an imaginary rebuke to his alleged personal interest in her.

It will be remembered that she also cited "implied contract" in her interview. She was well versed in current court cases— almost as well versed as Andrews was.

Legal Action: A Prolonged Process

With more and more employees beginning to wake up and sue for "unfair" or "unjust" dismissals, the employment at will doctrine is seen as "eroding" by some observers of the scene. One such is Charles G. Bakaly, Jr., a management attorney with O'Melveny & Myers, a Los Angeles law firm. At a meeting of the American Bar Association's Media Labor Law Seminar in Washington, he said that employers are being forced to make some "difficult decisions" about personnel policy in order to avoid suits charging unlawful discharge. "While an employer may still be able to terminate an employee at will 'for any reasons whatsoever,' it seems clear that courts will not allow the employer to act in an arbitrary manner."

Even so, for the employee who feels he or she has been terminated unfairly, it is not an easy prospect to bring suit against an employer. Even for the person protected by statute or under the umbrella of court precedents, it is a hard row to hoe. Most think two or three times before acting.

The advantage is still with the terminator. It takes time and money to sue. Such a case is a tort—a civil action of one person against a company charging wrongful action. Once the case is filed, the attorneys spend time interviewing witnesses. This is a legal process called "discovery."

Not until discovery is complete can the case be set for trial. It may take one or two years to finalize the proper interviews and prepare the case. For the person out of work, it is a difficult and costly ordeal.

Yet individuals today stand up to the strain in order to state their case before the world. The employer must realize that it is not so easy to push around employees as it once was. Most do. But at the same time management still argues that it must have the right to terminate workers for the good of the company.

The Right to Terminate at Will

Today's business world is a highly competitive one. Most Americans still believe in the right to hire and fire; the right to terminate the inefficient worker is part of the right of the efficient worker to take the vacated job and make good in it.

Yet plenty of unprotected workers today are fired unfairly, according to some students of the business scene. Jack Steiber, director of the school of labor and industrial relations at Michigan State University, feels that fully one-half of all terminated unprotected workers in the country are fired unfairly. He believes that "fifty thousand to one hundred thousand employees" could get their jobs back each year "if they had access to an impartial arbitration tribunal."

With only 20.9 percent of the work force today covered by collective bargaining agreements, there are consequently about eighty-five million private sector workers without the right of appeal of a discharge. According to Steiber, "Supervisors and managers are the largest group not organized and not protected." The typical unjustly terminated person with no right to appeal is "a white male, lower-level supervisory employee, under the age of forty."

Expanding the Precedents to Sue

Arthur Rosenfeld, a labor law attorney with the U.S. Chamber of Commerce, is not quite so sure that many Americans are terminated unfairly. "It's not that much of a problem," he says. "I have yet to see, despite all the figures, that there is a problem in the U.S. with unjust discharges."

An intensive search through the records of termination would show that an "incredibly" small number of discharges were for "immoral reasons" or otherwise unjustified, he notes. Arguing that reinstatement decisions may often result from technicalities—improper notice to an employee of termination and so on—and not from truly unjust discharge, he estimates that the true proportion of unjust terminations is probably about .01 percent.

As he puts it, unjust terminations are simply "not in the best interest of business." It is instead in the most selfish interests of management to uphold the morale of its employees. "An employer who develops a reputation of unfairly and unjustly terminating employees at a whim will be very hard-pressed to attract good employees."

Rosenfeld sees the employment at will and termination at will doctrine in a state of erosion, and he doesn't expect that erosion to "reverse or disappear." With a new direction set in court actions, "there are going to be attorneys who are going to take that precedent and expand it."

If the erosion continues, Rosenfeld predicts, it might be conceivable in the future for employers to bring suit against employees who terminate voluntarily and without cause. "I can come up with examples of employees quitting in which there was a moral justification to continue work because the employer was in the middle of a big order," he declares. "It is a two-way sword." Management so far has overlooked the other edge of the blade.

Even so, federal courts have been reluctant to take any cases involving termination at will. As Randy Alan Weiss, an attorney with Pierson, Ball and Dowd in Washington, D.C., points out, employees terminated are "more prone to bring cases in state courts as opposed to federal courts because federal courts acting as 'just another court of state' will look to existing state law and 'gag' chipping away at the common law doctrine of employment-at-will."

Such a move is highly unlikely at the present time, most labor-management authorities believe. The problem for the employer is not to dream of future moves that might smack of revenge but to try to clear up any gray areas in termination procedures, including preparation for discharge, periodic performance evaluations, and ongoing knowledge of the ways in which certain employees are protected, not only by statute but also by present court practice.

Helpful Hints to Managers on Terminations

The following checklist can help a supervisor or manager involved in the nasty business of terminations:

- Check carefully to ascertain the *real reason* for the termination. If it involves incompetence, obstreperousness, or inadequacy, or if it involves economic necessity, there should be no danger of lawsuit. If, however, it only *seems* to involve these problems and is really a matter of retaliation—for questioning an illegal company practice, for speaking out about a safety hazard, or for resistance to an invasion of privacy—the termination should be studied carefully and quite possibly reconsidered.

- Check carefully to see if any oral or written statements have been made to the employee that might create an implied employment contract that the termination could violate.
- If there is a possibility that the employee could make a case for retaliatory discharge, it would be wise to consult an attorney about the likely reactions of the state and federal courts in which the employee could bring suit. Points to consider might be:
  How broadly do the courts interpret "public policy"?
  How do the courts view a discharge that conflicts with the privileges of constitutents?
  What significance do the courts attach to a self-serving motive for discharge?
- Always treat any discharge as a liability event.
- Sanitize the hiring process and review employment applications and procedures for possible problems.
- Ensure that disciplinary procedures are clearly understood by employees and are conscientiously adhered to by management.
- Monitor supervisory performance evaluations and other documentation to ensure that they are honest and accurate.
- Be consistent in the future with past practice.
- Avoid terminations related to workers' compensation claims, service on a jury, testifying pursuant to a subpoena, or refusing to perform an illegal act.

CHAPTER 10

A Guide to Successful Termination

NOT EVERYONE can fire an employee with the aplomb of former British Prime Minister Harold Macmillan. The story goes that he had been through a long, involved soul search about one of his cabinet ministers and had decided the minister must go. After postponing the event because of its distasteful nature, Macmillan finally could stall no longer.

At the end of a brief interview, he edged the cabinet minister into the hallway and guided him to an old-fashioned elevator—one of those barred cages that descends into an open shaft. Timing his conversation with precision, Macmillan maneuvered his unsuspecting victim into the cage and pointed to the DOWN button.

When finally the minister had pushed the button, the gates had swung slowly closed, and the cage had begun to sink in the shaft, Macmillan told the man he was through. As the shocked victim moved slowly downward, his mouth gaping, his head sinking to the floor level, he cried out: "But why? Why?"

Macmillan leaned down toward the sinking cage. "Not good enough," he snapped.

Nor can anyone really employ the insouciance of the manager pictured in a recent cartoon on the firing of a subordinate: "Don't worry about it, Newton. Your work's fine. It's *you* we don't like."

Termination with Dignity and Sensitivity

A company's reputation as an employer depends on its ability to manage a termination with the least amount of resentment by the individual being separated, together with the greatest amount of understanding by the employees who remain. It is the aspect of sensitivity in the handling of the termination itself—not the reasons for the termination—that shapes the company attitude. In effect, termination is a public relations problem from the beginning to the end, a problem that affects the organization internally as well as externally.

One personnel chief of a *Fortune* 500 corporation puts it quite succinctly: "The first canon in terminating any employee is to treat him with maximum dignity. Try not to personalize the separation but restrict discussion to job performance. Don't talk about how someone parts his hair or how he dresses. Don't beat the guy up."

Interviews with dozens of personnel managers and high-echelon executives working for different types of corporations—both small and large—point up a woeful inadequacy in individual termination programs. Some companies do not have any established policy; executives who are responsible for firings are simply left to devise their own methods of operation. Other companies have shadowy policies that may be twisted and bent at will, depending on the particular situation.

Any company today that does not have some kind of established termination program—written or otherwise—is flirting with disaster, from a standpoint of both internal morale, external image, and legal consequences. The guidelines proposed here are an amalgam of many different systems, plus a few ideas turned up in discussions with various personnel directors. The guidelines fall into three basic divisions:

- Preparation
- Execution
- Wrap-up

Of these three, by far the most extensive and time-consuming is the first: preparation. To be effective, preparation should involve some 85 percent of the total effort by the terminator in the handling of the project. About 10 percent of the time and effort should be involved in the execution of the actual termination interview and perhaps 5 percent or less in the wrap-up of loose ends that gets things back to normal among the remaining employees.

The Many Aspects of Preparation

Preparation itself is neither a simple nor a unified phase of operation. It is a complex and multi-leveled problem. There are at least four main subdivisions to a good preparation scenario (although the importance of each of these elements varies from one dismissal to the next):

- Planning
- Documentation
- Scheduling
- Dress rehearsal

Planning

Planning involves a number of important points that must be decided upon before physically gathering together material for and moving into a termination. This stage could as well be called *prepreparation*, except that the term is repetitive and confusing. Planning usually involves making a number of decisions ahead of time that must be faced before going into action and setting up documentation.

For example, decisions must be made during this preliminary stage on five major issues:

1. Who is going to be the person to terminate the terminatee.
2. Whether there is going to be a third party involved in the termination interview.
3. Whether or not the terminatee should receive outplacement assistance.

4. An acceptable reason for the termination.
5. A proper cover story suitable both to the terminatee and to management.

Who Ties the Bell on the Cat?

A general rule of thumb followed by most companies is that the individual involved in the handling of a termination (that is, the terminator) should be the immediate superior of the person being terminated (that is, the terminatee).

The reason is fairly obvious. The immediate superior is the person who has probably selected the employee for hire. In the case of the long-time employee, that particular point obviously does not apply, since the individual who did the hiring may be long gone from the company. When the hirer is no longer available or is no longer the employee's immediate supervisor, the person's current immediate superior is the logical choice.

In the lower echelons of a corporation, where numbers of people work in a given department, the head of the department is usually the proper person to carry out a termination. This specific approach was used by both Don Riley and Mark Andrews in the case histories outlined in chapter 1. At these levels the problem of deciding who is to terminate the worker is a minor one. In the higher echelons of the company's executives—particularly in a small company that has only a handful of management personnel—that decision becomes difficult. In the case of a top management executive, the president of the company may take on the onerous burden himself or herself.

In some organizations the personnel department may become involved, but usually only as a backup element. That is, the personnel department may be able to provide documentation of an individual's failings or perhaps produce evaluation records to prove management's point.

Selecting the proper terminator usually does not involve a difficult decision. It is only somewhat touchy when it comes to finding a person to eliminate a management executive in a very high position.

Should a "Third Party" Be Involved?

For the lower-echelon worker, it is sometimes proper to include a third party during the final termination interview. Such a third party may be selected from the personnel department. This observer may be called in to back up the terminator if the case involved is a particularly sticky one in which vehement reactions can be expected from the terminatee.

With the typical employee, such an action is rarely required. In fact, the presence of a representative for management may immediately strike the terminatee as an unneeded bit of sadism that gives the scene the flavor of the Spanish Inquisition.

Nevertheless, in certain instances, the terminator may want an objective third party to oversee the procedure. In situations that might eventually involve litigation, the third party can act as a witness to whatever transpires at the interview.

Note that Mark Andrews did not choose to have a witness present when he dealt with Mary Healy in case history number 6. His reason for deciding against such a backup more or less parallels that of another executive with an enviable track record for being able to bring off terminations with a minimum of trouble, who has said:

> If you're thinking about having a third party present just to back you up, don't. I only had one situation in which I wished I had a witness. A secretary who had personal problems broke down when I told her she had to leave, and she became hysterical. That kind of thing happens only rarely.

Is Outplacement Assistance Necessary?

Another option the terminator must consider is that of including outplacement assistance for the terminated employee. Usually outplacement aid is reserved for high-echelon executives, but it can also be provided for middle-management executives if there is reason to believe the particular employee needs it.

Explained in detail in chapter 7, outplacement assistance is the use of an outside agent or agency to help an employer in the termination interview and help the employee in the moments and days that immediately follow termination. The actual purpose of outplacement is to locate a new job for the terminated employee with the least possible trauma for company and worker and in the shortest possible time.

The employer must consider the amount of money to be spent on outplacement assistance. While fairly expensive, such assistance may be worthwhile if the help involves an older worker or a highly placed individual who must be terminated through no fault of his or her own.

Generally the decision to involve an outplacer can be made by considering the specific pay schedule of the employee, as discussed in chapter 7.

The Reasons for the Termination

Assuming that the termination is being carried out for unsatisfactory performance or as part of a normal reduction in force, the terminator must marshall all the reasons leading to the decision to dismiss and put them into a clearly outlined, logical order. Not only must these be certain in the terminator's own mind, but he or she must be ready to explain them to the employee during the termination dialogue. These must be *real* reasons; they must be accurately defined; and they should never be simply cosmetic reassurances that have no meaning.

In some special cases it might be possible for the terminator to treat an older employee gently by telling a "little white lie," but in general it is risky to cover up the real reason for a termination. The distortion of fact can easily come back to haunt the terminator. Most details are easily presented—too much absenteeism, too little work, inability to do the job, inability to work with others—but some details are not easily discussed.

For example, it is difficult for the terminator to tell a worker that he or she is simply getting too old to handle the work. It is also a dangerous reason to use: the discharged employee can always claim the termination was dictated by age reasons. Old age cannot be used as the basis for discharge. If old age causes a person to fail at a job, the valid reason for termination should be unsatisfactory performance rather than old age. Senility itself is a health consideration, causing other legal problems, including possible suits for discrimination because of ill health or disability.

All factors leading up to a termination should be well laid out and discussed by management before being decided upon for use at the exit interview. These factors and the reasons for the termination must be accurately assembled and stated in unarguable terms. In addition, the terminator must be able to lay hands on written documentation to prove that performance or conduct has been unsatisfactory.

In termination due to a reduction in force, the terminator must make sure that all terminatees are selected according to seniority; otherwise a worker may challenge the termination and claim discrimination on one or various counts.

Considerations of seniority, performance, and behavior are covered in more detail in chapters 3, 4, and 5.

The Cover Story

Of utmost importance to the termination is the manner in which the news is communicated to the rest of the staff. Long before the termination interview, the terminator must prepare a logical, consistent, sensible story to tell not only to the people in the company but to others on the outside as well. The in-house story will be a prop to help management keep up morale; the external story will be a safety net for the terminated employee to help him or her get another job.

The cover story must be fair to both sides. It must not put the company in a bad light, nor should it put the employee in a position of looking incompetent or unruly. Although a good cover story should ideally be developed by both terminator and terminatee, this is usually not possible in the few moments allowed for the exit interview. Therefore, it is always wise for the terminator to draft such a story long before the termination date so that it will be available during the interview for the approval of the terminatee.

Such a story should be based on verifiable facts and details that do not run counter to the terminatee's character or known performance. It is obvious that such a story must be neither a total white lie nor a total black lie but must instead be put together with an eye toward not only the "way it plays in Peoria" but the actual truth involved.

No matter how it is formulated, and no matter what it says, such a cover story must be discussed and agreed upon by both parties before it is allowed to circulate either by word of mouth or in print.

The creation of the cover story involves several very critical decisions that must be made by the terminator:

1. Should the cover story tell exactly why the terminatee was fired?
2. How much detail should the terminator disclose about the findings that led to the termination?

3. How should the cover story be disseminated to company personnel?

Each case of termination is a law unto itself. No fixed rule can be stated to take care of the many possible variations. Generally speaking, however, there are several obvious rules of thumb.

One involves a cover story pertaining to a typical rif. The "why" of the story is a statement of the general cutback in personnel. The specific "why"—why terminatee A was selected over co-worker B—involves whether or not to mention work performance. In most companies co-workers know as much about the performance of their peers as management does, if not more. The worker whose performance is off is well known; the worker whose abilities are above average is equally well known. A simple statement of termination will suffice, without mentioning inferior performance.

Another situation might be termination for cause—that is, some matter of discipline the terminatee has ignored or flouted. In the majority of cases, such behavior is obvious to most of the person's co-workers. A brief explanation of the worker's nonconformance is all that is necessary.

However, if the disciplinary infraction is a serious one—theft, embezzlement, sexual abuse, bodily harm—then the cover story must be circumspectly phrased so as not to allow the terminatee to use it for legal purposes. A frank statement about such an infraction in a cover story would be immediately actionable. Again, a statement of the worker's termination is enough.

In another typical case—the case of termination for absenteeism—the terminatee's habit of being away from the job is usually evident to everyone who works around him or her. Such a cover story in fact *should* stress the terminatee's absences as the basis for termination; such a statement demonstrates that absenteeism will not be tolerated and will bolster the morale of those who have perfect or near-perfect attendance records. To pass over the obvious reason for dismissal would in effect tend to injure morale.

If the worker is really being let go because he or she is too old for the job, the cover story should usually concern itself with "early retirement." However, if the worker refuses to take early retirement, the terminator is immediately in a dilemma. If age is mentioned the terminatee may bring suit for discriminatory termination; if age is not mentioned, the terminatee can still bring suit, *claiming* discrimination. One possibility is for management to abolish the job and indicate in the cover story that the job is no more and that the worker has left for "lack of work." There is no hard and fast rule for this situation; the terminator must use his or her imagination to fabricate a reasonable scenario.

There are several points to watch out for when building a cover story:

- Never mention any reason for termination that may be actionable.
- Never mention any reason that could allow the terminatee to sue for discrimination.
- Never provide the remaining workers with an excuse to slack up on efficiency.

Later on we'll discuss how to disseminate the information in the cover story to the rest of the company's personnel.

Documentation

Documentation involves two main points that must be taken care of long before the exit interview. One is a detailed rundown on the severance package being offered to the terminated employee; the other is a complete and accurate file of the employee's evaluation papers, performance charts, and any other documents pertaining to behavior during his or her stay at the company.

The Severance Package

The severance package must be prepared by the terminator considerably prior to the exit interview. Actually, the real work is done by the finance department or by whoever is in charge of financial arrangements in the company. If there is a clear-cut set of rules and regulations pertaining to severance benefits, they can easily be followed in making up the severance package. If there are no clear-cut rules, the terminator and the financial manager must work the details out together.

The severance package must be planned at this stage so that its later presentation will be comprehensive and understandable at a glance. Questions should be anticipated by the terminator in the planning stage, so that answers can be prepared by the financial manager. The terminator should have at hand such details as the place to go for unemployment benefits, the amount of the benefits, whether or not the company will continue medical insurance and for how long, and so on.

For the terminator who has worked long and hard with the financial department to prepare a good severance package, it might seem a temptation to take pride in the company's generosity and to ask the terminated employee whether or not he or she thinks the package is fair.

This is an absolute no-no, even if the terminator wants a genuine reaction in order to guide him or her in future severance preparations. The immediate reaction of the terminated employee might be to flare up and say something like this: "Oh, it's a lovely package! And you know what you can do with it!"

Nonfinancial Severance Perks

Besides cash support, the terminator should have all non-economic benefits or perks planned in detail. The terminator must discuss with management such details as whether or not the former employee can use the office to work on his or her résumé and conduct the job hunt as well as what kind of reference the terminatee can expect from the employer.

The terminator must decide how to close out any projects the terminatee has been working on or is working on at the time of the dismissal, so that no work will be left hanging in the air at the terminatee's departure.

One executive comments on termination preparation in this manner:

> Outline the help that will be forthcoming for the fired person, such as office, telephone, [and] secretarial support, if any; outplacement counseling; and policy on references. . . . Cover any severance and vacation payments, arrangements on insurance benefits, and any instructions covering the return of any keys, credit cards, and other company materials or funds due. If the firing is the result of an overall reduction in the company's work force, this should, of course, be cited as the reason for termination.

Documentation of Reasons for Termination

It is mandatory that the terminator be able to back up all reasons given for termination with documentary proof. During the planning stage he or she should therefore collect all time clock cards, attendance records, evaluation sheets, review papers, reprimands, warnings, and any other type of written notices to make up a package of proof to be produced at the time of the exit interview.

These papers should support in every way possible the specific reasons given by the terminator for the separation. The presence of the actual papers at the exit interview will go a long way toward cooling the ardor of the belligerent worker if a dramatic and contentious scene begins to build.

No reference need be made to the documentation in the event the interview proceeds quietly and with decorum. If there are any rebuttal statements, any denials of facts, any challenges to the terminator's claims, the actual points of the charges may be read aloud. Usually this has the effect of defusing the employee's uptightness.

Documentation will also come in handy if a worker decides to bring the termination to the attention of a grievance committee, or to some outside organization like the EEOC, or into the court system on the grounds that it has been unfair or discriminatory.

Scheduling

When the terminator has made all preliminary decisions and has collected all pertinent documentary evidence necessary to back up the termination, he or she must then set about scheduling the date and place of the actual termination interview.

Setting the Proper Time for the Exit Interview

Timing is extremely important in this type of situation. Not only is the hour of the day important but the day of the week and the month of the year as well.

What Hour and Day?

According to the most modern approach to termination, the deed should usually be done:

• During the morning, when both terminator and terminatee are fresh and able to cope with adversity.

• On Monday, Tuesday, or Wednesday—but *never on Friday!*

"It's depressing for the fired employee to have to go home on a Friday without a job," says one business executive. "Early in the week a person has more strength to take that kind of thing."

The rationale is uncomplicated. The employee who has been terminated late Friday afternoon has plenty of time to go home and brood about the treatment accorded by the company. These churning, negative thoughts can build up over the weekend, with recollections of bad scenes between employee and employer and with gradually increasing rancor.

The dismissed employee has two days in which to feel more and more abandoned and alienated. By late Sunday, the terminatee may begin telephoning friends, either in the company or out of it, to spread the word about the "unjust" dismissal. With each conversation, a little more vitriol creeps into the diatribe, resulting in the spread of a great many malignant rumors about the company.

It is during this crucial weekend period that many cast-off employees decide to sue the company for discrimination or hurt it in some specific way. Many come up with ingenious schemes, which they later pursue—both to their own detriment and to the detriment of the company.

The rationale for firing early in the morning is also quite logical. It is a time when people are generally fresher, more rested, and better able to deal with adversity. The emotion stirred by the action of termination can almost immediately be translated into energy for use in a positive direction in trying to locate another job.

In the afternoon, an employee is generally tired and sometimes short-tempered. The mood is completely wrong for an added dimension of trouble.

The Case of Randy White

Let's return to case history number 1—the termination of Randy White by Don Riley. Riley, who timed his terminations for Friday afternoon, thought his troubles were over as he headed home for a quiet weekend. In fact, Riley's traumatic moments of Friday afternoon were only a prelude to a much more troublesome weekend.

On Saturday the repercussions of his actions began to sound in his own home. Early in the morning, while the Rileys were having a quiet breakfast before visiting their daughter in a nearby suburb, Eve White, Randy's wife, phoned Pamela Riley. Shortly after the conversation ended, Pamela was back at the breakfast table in a bitter argument with her husband.

Eve White was in tears, Pamela reported. All evening she had listened to a series of diatribes against Atlas Industries by her outraged husband. Now Randy was on the telephone calling up friends at other companies and at Atlas, too, telling everyone how miserably he had been treated. He was mad at the president and mad at Riley. He was threatening to sue the company.

In the afternoon the president of the company, having just received a vitriolic call from Randy White, phoned Riley and castigated him for encouraging White to accost him by phone. When Riley pointed out that he had never encouraged his former assistant to contact the president, the company head blew up and told Riley that he had bungled the termination badly—handling it ineptly and stupidly.

But that wasn't the end of it. On Monday, Atlas was the scene of chaos and rhetorical bloodshed. Randy White was wandering around the corridors bothering all his peers with complaints and making snide remarks about Atlas. He spent most of the week on the telephone bad-mouthing Atlas and only coincidentally trying to get another job.

Actually, Randy White hurt himself as much as he hurt Atlas with his antics. But the fundamental error was essentially Don Riley's: partly in scheduling the termination interview for a Friday afternoon and partly in allowing the terminatee to use the premises "until he got another job."

What Time of Year?

As to the time of year to terminate, usually the employer has little choice in the matter. Business downturns occur at any time; if a rif must be effected, an employer simply can't wait for the proper month. However, if there is a choice in the matter, the best month from the employee's standpoint would be January.

A survey conducted to determine the most favorable months for positive responses to mail campaigns by job seekers has determined the following order of the twelve months of the year, with the positive percentages included, from 1 to 100:

January	100	April	75
February	95	September	75
March	90	May	70
October	90	December	70
August	85	July	60
November	80	June	50

If possible, it would seem that an employer might be doing an employee a favor (of sorts) by terminating in January, February, March, or October, with the months of June, July, December, and May to be avoided. June and July are bad months because of vacations; August is the beginning of a pickup to October. January, February, and March are good in some cases because winter brings about a certain amount of stability in the job market—paying up Christmas debts, staying on the job while the weather is bad, and so on.

Selecting the Proper Place for Termination

Almost as important as the selection of the proper time for the exit interview is the selection of the proper place. Assuming that the final interview is to be conducted one-on-one—with only two people involved—it should be conducted in a private and quite place. The location should be a dignified one—possibly a conference room or an office that is not being used.

The exit interview should never be conducted by the terminator in his or her own office. Even when there can be no interruptions, there is an advantage to being in another site for the termination. At the end of the discussion, the employer can simply stand up and leave the office, indicating that the interview is over. If the terminator is in his or her own office and a nasty situation develops, or if the employee wants to argue and harangue, the terminator has little chance to stroll out and end the discussion: it's his or her own office!

Aside from certain cases, discussed earlier, in which the presence of a third party may be deemed advisable, the exit interview should be conducted in private, with no one else aware of the nature of the dialogue.

Dress Rehearsal

The fourth and last division of the preparation stage is that of the so-called dress rehearsal. This involves a run-through of the termination interview with a disinterested party in order to see if the preliminary preparations have been adequately handled.

Dress Rehearsal

No terminator should ever assume that he or she will be able to conduct a satisfactory exit interview without running through the specific words and gestures to be used beforehand. The actual mechanics of telling an employee that he or she is no longer employed and must look for another job is never easy, even when softened by smooth-flowing phrases.

No terminator can ever bring off a satisfactory termination unless he or she has already thought through the wording in advance. To wing it at a termination is to crash and burn.

The best plan is to write up a one-sided dialogue, covering all the facts of the matter. These facts should be stated in a straightforward, concise fashion. They should proceed along the specific lines discussed under the second major section below, which deals with execution.

A Little Street Theater Improvisation

Even the greatest of playwrights know that the most carefully crafted and beautiful lines ever written on paper may not sound quite so beautiful or carefully crafted when uttered by the human voice. Likewise, words that look cold and dead on paper may become soaring tributes to the muses when uttered aloud. It is difficult for people today—with word processors and typewriters in every office—to understand that before the written word there was the spoken word.

It is the spoken word that becomes important in the termination interview. It is never quite the same in the utterance as in the imagination. One executive says:

> I never fire anybody without practicing beforehand. I call in someone who doesn't even know the projected victim and set up a little improvisation. We pretend we're going through a termination interview. I'm the terminator, and he's the one being terminated. You'd be surprised what you learn about your planned message when it comes down to a one-on-one situation. You begin to stammer and turn red, and you also tend to be harsher

and more vindictive than you plan to be. A dry run is a must. I simply can never write a termination script without changing it when I go over it with another employee.

This executive's message makes good sense. No terminator ever knows what is going to happen once he or she gets in that room with the person to be terminated. Even with a letter-perfect script, the dialogue can go way out of line. The emphasis may be wrong; unanticipated responses can be stunning surprises. Even with all the carefully prepared documents, the whole interview may become a shambles because of a lack of foresight.

Practice doesn't always make perfect, but it does help point the way to perfection. The termination interview will be that much better if it has had a dry run before the actual production. A give-and-take rehearsal between people acting out roles can show up defects in a script or a scenario that simply refuses to play.

Execution of the Exit Interview

At this point, the preparation phase of the termination is over and done. It is time now to move on to the actual execution of the termination. As has been explained, this usually takes no more than ten to fifteen minutes and must be done with precision, clarity, and dignity.

In spite of all the preliminary work, the mind-set of the terminator must be delicately tuned to the ordeal ahead and must be adjusted properly in order to anticipate and cope with any eventuality.

Be Prepared for Any Contingency

It is essential that the terminator anticipate unusual reactions from the worker to be terminated. Whether or not they actually do come about is beside the point. Overanticipation is better than underanticipation.

The terminator who fears possible violence, heart attack, or hysterical outburst is usually exaggerating the situation. However, such responses are not unheard of and should always be considered as remote possibilities.

In some cases it is likely that the employee will react with hostility, anger, and insulting remarks. To cope with such reactions, the terminator must always keep a cool head and steady hand. The employee may well be baiting the terminator, trying to trigger a remark that could later be used to demonstrate unfairness, discrimination, or another type of actionable intention.

A clever employee trying to bait an employer might blurt out: "You're firing me because I'm better than Marjorie—but I've seen the way you look at her!" The best thing for the terminator to do is to remain cool and expressionless. "I'm sorry you feel that way, Betty, but the decision still stands." That firm response should be enough. It can be repeated in many different ways.

The attitude of Mark Andrews in case history number 6 is a good example of a terminator faced with a belligerent and challenging terminatee. The attempts Mary Healy made to bait Andrews were almost endless; Andrews managed to hold his temper and thus kept control of the conversation.

In marked contrast is Don Riley's flare-up during the interview in case history number 2, that with Arthur Mason. Not only was Riley unprepared with documentation or through preliminary work, but he was unable to keep the interview on a proper track during its execution.

Once again, it is the terminator's mind-set that is important during the first few moments of the exit interview. Firm control, confident attitude, and cool behavior are absolute essentials. Naturally, in order to be able to maintain a cool exterior, the proper preparation must have been done ahead of time, as has been noted time and again.

The Three Elements of the Exit Interview

The exit interview itself, while short and concise, must be thoroughly prepared and rehearsed, as has been explained. In execution, the interview breaks down into these segments:

- Statement of termination.
- Documentation to back it up.
- Creation of the cover story.

Statement of Termination

The main consideration and purpose of the exit interview is simple and concise: it is for the terminator to tell the terminatee that he or she has been terminated and will no longer work for the company. The terminator must make it crystal-clear that the decision by management is final and cannot be reversed. He or she must also tell the terminatee the basic facts: the effective date of departure and the manner in which the employee is expected to clean out personal belongings and vacate the premises.

"Termination is the time for a clear, concise statement explaining that the decision has been made, has been approved all the way up the line and is irrevocable," says one personnel executive.

The statement of termination usually involves five main points:

- Announcement of termination.
- The reasons for it.
- The fact that the decision is irrevocable.
- The severance package (financial).
- The severance package (nonfinancial, if any).

Don't Beat around the Bush!

Of crucial importance is a basic rule of thumb in carrying out the termination interview: *Keep it brief and keep it clear.*

It is not out of line to establish a time limit of from ten to fifteen minutes for the exit interview. Considering the number of years an employee has worked for a company, it is perhaps short shrift, but there is no reason for the interview to last any longer. All five basic points mentioned above can easily be covered in that time. Any arguments and rejoinders can be cut short—and should be. Hemming and hawing may *seem* to soften the blow, but the truth of the matter is that *nothing* can really soften such a blow.

"There's no reason to go into the details of each and every malfeasance," one employment counselor says. "These should have been covered more properly in earlier sessions in which the employee would have been informed of management's unhappiness and told exactly how performance could be upgraded and by when."

There is simply no excuse for cluttering up an exit interview with platitudes—evasive statements of sympathy that simply cloud the issue. The fact of the termination is the main point under discussion; adding platitudes to try to soften the blow does nothing but slow down the pace of the interview.

Beating around the bush also tends to obscure the real point of the dialogue. Be absolutely certain that the fired person leaves the termination interview with a clear understanding that he or she has been fired!

One termination consultant relates a bizarre situation in which a terminated individual left the interview with a clear understanding that she had just been promoted! The employer, trying to make the meeting easy, had emphasized all the positives: "A great opportunity." "Best for you." "You'll do much better." The phrases "You're not going to be working here any longer" or "You're fired" had never been uttered.

The Decision Is Irrevocable

A cantankerous employee may try to rebut an implication of laziness or inadequacy by repeating a long litany of accomplishments, assignments, and exceptionally well done jobs, with a plaintive, "You know I'm good at the job. Why am I going when Rogers and Thomas are staying? I'll put my record up against theirs any day!"

The only way to answer such a complaint is: "I hear you, but the decision is irrevocable." The fatal error in such an exchange is for the terminator to go on the defensive; from the moment the interview is out of his or her control, the termination is a shambles.

Another ploy that should be anticipated is the instant attempt to make a deal, to bargain for another spot. "I understand the problem in your department, but can't I be transferred to accounting? They need a secretary there. I know there's no need for a knowledge of bookkeeping. And you know I'm a good typist." The answer to this kind of pleading is for the terminator to have in hand a concise, noninflammatory, kindly answer: "We already approached all the departemtns in the company. Your name was discussed but your qualifications don't fit the changed job specifications."

If the individual being terminated should suddenly burst into tears, the employer must stay aloof as best he or she can, using the outburst to try to draw off the anger and the fear by weathering the crying and sniffling in the best possible manner. It is much easier to write instructions about "weathering crying" than it is to accomplish the task; nevertheless, it is the only to bring off a successful termination interview.

In effect, weeping does tend to act as a catharsis to the pain and suffering caused by the rejection implied in the termination. Both terminator and terminatee should feel relieved of the tension once the spell is over.

A Look at Insensitivity

One of the most off-putting ways of trying to handle a termination interview is to objectify the meeting to such an extent that it becomes completely inhuman.

Note the insensitivity in Don Riley's statement to Arthur Mason in case history number 2: "You've never really put your shoulder to the wheel in this organization. It's time you got out."

Riley's insensitivity involves not only his attitude toward Mason but his almost total disregard of the activities and record of his employee.

"I was mistaken in hiring you in the first place," he goes on to say. "And when I found out how mistaken I was, I should have fired you immediately."

If he *did* note Mason's shortcomings, why, indeed, did he not fire him then and there?

Mason's response—"I've heard no complaints!"—hit the nail right on the head.

The Failure to Keep Performance Records

Riley was also lax in not determining Mason's severance package. But of course, Riley's most important mistake was in completely forgetting the incident of the faulty airplane valve, which Arthur Mason had criticized forcefully.

What Riley failed to do was to tell Mason the truth: there was, in fact, an effort to reduce the number of personnel in the department. Mason's inability to get on with his co-workers made him a perfect target for termination. Riley's failure to keep records on his employees' work performance was the fatal flaw.

As for ordering Mason to clean out his desk and be out of the office by the end of the day, it was not an unusual request to make, nor was it particularly surprising.

What was surprising was Riley's inability to control his temper. He began to falter when Mason reminded him of the incident of the faulty valve; then, with Riley fussing and fuming, Mason deliberately twisted the knife by threatening to take company secrets to a competitor. At that, Riley completely blew up and *personalized* his own animosity toward Mason with a very unprofessional insult ending with: "I wouldn't give you a wooden nickel for any information in that head of yours!"

Such an outburst usually plays into the hands of the employee, allowing him or her the luxury of a counterthrust coupled with an expression of rage. In fact, Mason himself stalked out at that point—giving him, essentially, the "last word" in the argument, which, even though it was a silent one, was more effective than Riley's personalized insult.

How to Keep the Parting Brief

Contrast Riley's inept performance with Andrews's well-documented and well-prepared exit interview with Dick Barton. Note how carefully Andrews has prepared his opening statement:

> Dick, I'm sorry this hasn't worked out. Your evaluation sheets show that you are a worker with his heart in the right place, but you are simply unable to perform with the consistency that we need at this company. When you disappeared two weeks ago, there was insufficient staff prepared for a major convention. You know this is your responsibility. Along with your reliability, your attendance is also a major problem.

Such a remark can easily close the terminator's opening statement, leaving any reaction up to the employee.

The Ball in the Employee's Court

Once the statement of termination is complete, the terminator waits for some response. The terminatee may have little to say. However, some employees in such a situation have a great deal to say, as did Mary Healy in case history number 6. When she acted flippant and indifferent with Andrews, he immediately responded with a listing of her shortcomings and the following remark:

> You've gone through all the possible steps in our appeal procedure, Mary. You have consistently and blatantly refused to obey the rules here concerning absenteeism. I must therefore tell you that you are being terminated as of today. You have two weeks' severance pay, which you can pick up at finance.

At this point the exit interview moves on into the second phase: the presentation of written documentation.

Documentation

Although it may not be necessary in every exit interview to confront the terminatee with papers to prove management's point, the terminator must be prepared to do so. If necessary, he or she should be able to go over the points one by one, with the help of the supporting papers, thus building management's case.

As has been pointed out, once the documentation is in evidence, it is usually enough to quiet down the most obstreperous of objecting terminatees, although in some instances the arguments may persist. The skilled terminator must know when to cut off further argument and move on to the next phase, which is the discussion of the cover story.

The Cover Story

The creation of the cover story has already been considered. It is at this point in the exit interview that the terminator produces a draft of the cover story and discusses it with the terminatee.

In the event that the interview has gone along without much antipathy, it is quite probable that the dismissed employee will agree to the cover story as it has been outlined, with perhaps a detail altered here or there.

However, in the event that the confrontation has been full of animosity, the discharged employee may not agree to it at all. In that case, it is up to the terminator and the terminatee to come to some sort of rapprochement on the spot and create a cover story that will satisfy all concerned.

Checklist for Managing the Exit Interview

- Minimize uncertainty, rumor, and speculation by spelling out the actual facts and circumstances that have led to the termination.
- Develop the facts in a step-by-step, logical manner. Do not be abrupt and terse.
- Allow the individual to ask questions and to make observations pertinent to the case.
- Review written documentation pertaining to performance-based termination criteria.
- Explain the proposed cover story the company will provide to executives of other companies when they call to check employment references. If unsatisfactory, work out a substitute cover story with the employee.
- Offer a concise, clear, and understandable rundown on severance pay and severance perks and explain any other assistance available to the employee.
- If applicable, explain outplacement counseling services or other assistance available.
- Seek the employee's reactions and feelings regarding his or her performance, career, and departure.
- Focus on the future of the individual and provide constructive help and guidance. Do not dwell on the past.

The Wrap-up of the Termination

At the conclusion of the exit interview, the terminator must perform two more functions:

- Compose a memo of termination.
- Disseminate the cover story to the company.

Memorandum of Termination

Immediately upon closing the exit interview, the terminator should write a memorandum covering the details of the dialogue. It should be composed when the terminator's memory is fresh. This record is extremely important in the event there are appeals or challenges following the termination.

In the memo the terminator should repeat verbatim what was said, by whom, and how and include descriptions of the emotional tone of both terminator and terminatee.

If other events transpire after the termination interview, these facts should be included in the memorandum. If the termination should be challenged and brought either to arbitration or to the courts, such a memo will prove invaluable to the company's management representative.

News of the Termination

The termination is not yet over. Although the terminator and the terminatee have agreed upon a cover story to tell to employees, friends, and future employers, the actual situation in the company itself has not yet been wrapped up satisfactorily. Because in many cases the discharged employee does not immediately return to his or her co-workers, many of them may not know that the individual has been fired.

The last step in the wrap-up of the termination is for the terminator to broadcast the pertinent information about the termination among the co-workers of the former employee. This dissemination of information may be done by memo, which can be handed out to members of the staff, or by word of mouth if the division or department is small.

Actually, the terminator may use both methods simultaneously. Word of mouth spreads rapidly in any company. For those who miss that news in its rapid form—by being outside the office at an off-site meeting or perhaps on vacation—the memo is a good backup method of presenting such information.

The announcement—verbal or written—should be couched in quick, concise terms that do not raise questions or cast aspersions:

Peter Johnson has left the company as of July 19. His replacement will be announced as soon as the choice has been confirmed.

In the Final Analysis . . .

"Finally, remember two things," one outplacement consultant warns about terminations:

It's okay to fire, and it's okay to be fired. It's never easy for a supervisor to do or for an employee to accept. But it need never be an appetite- and sleep-losing experience. It can be a vast relief on both sides. And the majority of fired people we work with in outplacement grow and improve their personal and career status as a direct result of having been let go. As Thomas Jefferson wrote in 1792: "A man who qualifies himself well for his calling never fails of employment in it."

One supervisor/manager says:

When you fire someone, avoid being unnecessarily cruel. Look for some true or credible reason to explain the termination—one that does not hurt his feelings too much and lets him keep his self-respect and pride when he leaves.

Once the final decision has been taken to fire an employee, do it at once; procrastination doesn't help anybody. Prefer offering him two weeks' termination pay instead of two weeks' notice. A fired worker's efficiency—which was anyway very low and very bad—becomes nonexistent during the notice weeks, so it is better to get rid of him at once.

One student of termination measures offers the following recommendations:

I am suggesting that more managers and their companies recognize the inevitability of executive job termination and propose to deal with it in the most enlightened and compassionate manner possible. More companies should follow the lead of those that have established enlightened policies and procedures for dismissing managers and executives. Recognizing that they cannot guarantee job security, these progressive companies provide dismissed executives with emotional and practical security during the traumatic transitional period. Such security can take many forms, including the use of an office and secretarial support, underwriting professional placement, and the reasonable continuity of salary and benefits. Through such measures, an increasing number of companies are assuring that their executives enjoy some of the "perks" that their union workers do.

Reviewing the Steps in Termination

Firing a subordinate is one of those grim chores that may come up at any time in the business world. Although it can never be a thing to be proud of, a termination can be a considerate and humane parting of the ways, done with style and grace, with firmness and determination, and overlaid with compassion and sympathy.

Nevertheless, there are booby traps and pitfalls into which the unwary terminator may stumble. Let's take a trip back through the various subjects covered in this book, with an overall look at the problems involved in firing a subordinate—and the ways in which the terminator can avoid or forestall trouble.

When an employee becomes eligible for discharge—whether it be for an ordinary reduction in force or for on-the-job inadequacy of any kind—the terminator should first of all check through the company's personnel policies to find out if there is a set of rules and regulations to be followed regarding termination.

If there are none—which may be the case in the average small or medium-size company—the terminator should then discuss the situation with officers in the company responsible for and knowledgeable about personnel matters. Whatever advice he or she may discover should immediately be acted upon or stored for future use.

Checking for Such Considerations as "Implied Contract," "Malicious Termination," and "Public Policy"

If the corporate personnel policy leaves the terminator free to go ahead as he or she pleases, the terminator should then check carefully to see if any oral or written statements might have been made to the employee implying any kind of employment "contract."

If no such implied contract can be construed, the terminator should continue searching through the employee's background to make sure that there are no hidden elements or actions that might be used by the employee to argue that the "real reason" for the dismissal wasn't economic necessity or on-the-job inadequacy but retaliation of some kind. Case history number 3, that of Monica Henry, shows the type of problem that might arise.

Such retaliation might also be for questioning some illegal company practice; for speaking out publicly about some safety hazard, either in the company or in one of its products, as in case history number 2, that of Arthur Mason; or for resisting an invasion of privacy.

Checking for Statutory Considerations

The terminator should also be cognizant of the possibility that discriminatory dismissal could be charged on the basis of statutory provisions regarding sex, minority rights, age, or disability. One such charge discussed was, of course, that of Randy White in case history number 1—the charge of age discrimination.

Any company officer involved in termination should keep constantly in mind current judicial decisions regarding discrimination in termination. The courts are changing constantly in their overall outlook on the rights of employees; the possibility of lawsuits must always be faced by any terminator.

Before proceeding, the terminator should explore the possibility that any such challenge might be forthcoming. If so, he or she should consult an attorney about the likely findings of state or federal courts where the employee might sue.

Preparing the Termination Scenario

Once these preliminary explorations have been carefully conducted, the terminator should proceed to draw up his or her own termination scenario.

He or she should first of all study any possible considerations of seniority, to see how they apply to the particular employee. In a similar vein, the terminator should study the performance of the employee, along with his or her behavior—collecting all pertinent documents for possible use to counteract any future challenges to the termination.

If the company has any kind of appeal system, the terminator must make sure that it is in working order and that the terminator's case is well prepared and ready for presentation. If there is no appeal system, the terminator should be prepared to present evidence of the company's case against the employee if the employee brings up the matter before a professional arbitrator.

At this point, the terminator must proceed with his or her own dismissal package. This includes the planning, execution, and wrap-up considerations of the exit interview.

The most important part of the planning phase involves the preparation of the severance package, including special perks as well as cash benefits, which must be worked out in detail before the exit interview so that once the interview is complete, there is no need for further communication between terminator and terminatee. A proper cover story should be prepared as well.

Executing the Exit Interview

The terminator should also rehearse his or her termination dialogue with a disinterested fellow employee in order to iron out any wrinkles in its presentation. When all preparation is complete, the terminator should prepare for the final interview by having all necessary papers in hand and a clear-cut picture of the employee's background in mind.

By telling the employee exactly why he or she is being terminated, what will be offered in the way of cash and other benefits, and how the dismissal story will be handled, the terminator should be able to wind up the termination interview in from ten to fifteen minutes.

The most important consideration in the execution of the interview is the mind-set of the terminator. He or she must be thoroughly positive about the reasons for termination, have cleared his or her mind of all guilt about the termination, and be able to rebut any arguments on the part of an obstreperous employee without losing his or her cool or control of the dialogue.

Proper execution of the exit interview should lead to a quick wrap-up, including preparation of a memorandum of dismissal and dissemination of the cover story regarding the employee's termination to the rest of the company's workers.

With all these points in mind, the terminator should be able to accomplish an effective termination interview—an exit dialogue that carries with it a minimum of hard feelings on the part of the terminatee and a minimum of guilt on the part of the terminator.